Pennsylvania TRAIL OF HISTORY® COOKBOOK

The Editors of
STACKPOLE BOOKS
and
**THE PENNSYLVANIA
HISTORICAL AND MUSEUM
COMMISSION**

Foreword by
WILLIAM WOYS WEAVER

STACKPOLE BOOKS

PENNSYLVANIA HISTORICAL
AND MUSEUM COMMISSION

Published by
STACKPOLE BOOKS
5067 Ritter Road
Mechanicsburg, PA 17055
www.stackpolebooks.com

Printed in the United States of America

10 9 8 7 6 5 4 3 2 1

FIRST EDITION

Edited by
Kyle R. Weaver, Stackpole Books
Diane B. Reed, Pennsylvania Historical and Museum Commission

Sidebar text by
Diane B. Reed and Fred Lauver, Pennsylvania Historical and Museum Commission

Cover design by
Caroline Stover

Photography
Craig A. Benner: cover, vi, vii, ix, x, xii
David J. Healy: v
Kyle R. Weaver: ii

All other credits noted throughout

Printed on recycled paper

Library of Congress Cataloging-in-Publication Data

Pennsylvania trail of history cookbook / the editors of Stackpole Books and the Pennsylvania Historical and Museum Commission ; foreword by William Woys Weaver.
        p.   cm.
    Includes index.
    ISBN 0-8117-3144-8
    1. Cookery, American.   2. Cookery—Pennsylvania.   3. Historic sites—Pennsylvania.   I. Pennsylvania Historical and Museum Commission.
TX715.P462   2004
641.59748—dc22
                                                        2004006319

Contents

Breads (continued)

Main Dishes

Main Dishes *(continued)*

Vegetables and Sides

Desserts

Desserts (continued)

Beverages

Features

Foreword

It is really thrilling to be able to eat one's way across a state, especially one as long across and as historically rich as Pennsylvania. I cannot think of another place in America where we can taste the seventeenth-century flavors of a Swedish log cabin, the baroque delights of grand country houses, the steaming simplicity of coal miners' kitchens, the fare of oil fields, cloisters, or such politically important sites as Washington's Crossing or Bushy Run Battlefield. It's a delight to see how the inventive personnel at each of the twenty-six historically important sites represented in this cookbook have brought their own particular foods into line with period interpretation and site context. Many visitors to our Pennsylvania museum sites are welcomed by the aromas of living history when they walk into the kitchens of these wonderful old buildings; now they can take those memories home with them and enjoy the food firsthand.

No other state in America can claim the rich variety of regional dishes that have evolved in Pennsylvania; more than 100 foods are distinctive to the greater Philadelphia region alone, and that takes in only one small part of the state. So it is with great pleasure that I find many local specialties in this cookbook: dandelion salad, a perennial favorite; pickled red beets; chicken corn soup; mush muffins; buckwheat griddle cakes; scrapple; shad prepared in several ways; and colcannon—where would the coal miners have been without it? There also are several fun regional foods, such as snickerdoodles and ring-a-lings; kids love them, and kids learning about the past is one important reason this cookbook is such a valuable teaching tool. I can certainly see these recipes finding a useful place in public school history programs. While it is an excellent salute to our Keystone State, this handy manual is also a salute to the hardworking staffs of all the historic sites involved for their dedication in preserving our state's rich culinary heritage.

William Woys Weaver
Roughwood
Devon, Pennsylvania

Editors' Preface

This collection of wonderful, diverse recipes from the history of the Keystone State is the result of a rich collaboration between Stackpole Books and the Pennsylvania Historical and Museum Commission (PHMC). The two bodies first came together to produce the Pennsylvania Trail of History Guides, a series of handbooks on the museums and historic sites administered by the Commonwealth of Pennsylvania. As this monumental project began to reach its completion, it then seemed natural to develop a cookbook to not only compile the characteristic recipes from the twenty-six Trail of History sites, but also to document the unique foodways of the various people from the many ethnic, religious, and occupational groups who have inhabited the state.

Within this book are the foods that were prepared and eaten by Native Americans on the early frontier, guests of the Penn Family at Pennsbury Manor, soldiers in the Revolutionary War, sailors aboard the U.S. Brig *Niagara*, miners in the anthracite region, and passengers on the great railroads of the twentieth century. With each recipe, the providing site is identified after the instructions. All of the recipes have been adapted for the modern kitchen and tested.

As a collaborative effort, the cookbook owes its existence to the hard work and dedication of a large number of people. The book was conceived and created by Stackpole Books in cooperation with the PHMC's Division of Publications and Bureau of Historic Sites and Museums. Donna Williams heads the latter, and she and her staff have reviewed the text and the recipes for historic accuracy.

Thanks to staff, volunteers, and friends of the Pennsylvania Historical and Museum Commission sites and the Pennsylvania State Archives who provided recipes, foodways, and encouragement for this cookbook, including Janet Banks, Andrea Bashore, Kurt Bell, Michael Bertheaud, Anita Blackaby, Carrie Blough, Jean Karinch Brooks, Dolores Buchsen, Jane Budinger, Lori D. Burke, Marion Campbell, Toni Collins, Brooke Dearman, Rita Dobson, David Dubick, David Dunn, Sherry Felske, Amy Killpatrick Fox, Charles Fox, Ann Gayetty, Nada Gray, Troy Grubb, Kelly Hackman, Jerri Horner, Marcia Houston, Beatrice Hulsberg, Robert Johnson, Hilary Krueger, Chester Kulesa, Mary Ann Landis, Emily Lapisardi, William Leech, James Lewars, Steve Ling, Beverly Manbeck, Thomas Martin, Carol and John Marymont, Michelle Matz, John Meyer, Douglas Miller, Stephen Miller, Irene Mokwa, Patricia Mousley, Michael J. O'Malley III, Susan McLellan Plaisted, Howard Pollman, Deborah Reddig, Linda Ries, Stefan Rohal, Walter Rybka, Elizabeth Rump, 60th Royal Americans, Willis Shirk, Virginia Sinn, Marcy Slater, Robert Smilek, Chuck Smith, Stephen Somers, Ema Trump, Martha Van Atta, Louis Waddell, Esther Walter, Mark Ware, Mark Weber, Carolyn Wodzinski, Kelly Young, and Barbara Zolli.

The following professionals deserve thanks for their essential roles: Art Becker (photographer), Craig A. Benner (photographer), Joyce Bond (copy editor), Amy Cooper (associate editor), Cathy Craley (production manager), Roxy Hambleton (proofreader), Kerry Jean Handel (designer and paginator), David J. Healy (photographer), Alice Martin (typist), Beth Oberholtzer (paginator), Tracy Patterson (original designer), David Reisch (editorial assistant), and Caroline Stover (cover designer).

And special thanks to food historian William Woys Weaver for offering the insightful words that introduce this book and his support and counsel to the editors.

Kyle R. Weaver
Stackpole Books

Diane B. Reed
*Pennsylvania Historical
and Museum Commission*

Pennsylvania TRAIL OF HISTORY® COOKBOOK

Appetizers, Relishes, Salads, and Pickles

Warm Cabbage and Grape Salad

1 head of cabbage
salt
3 strips of bacon, diced
³/₄ cup apple cider vinegar
1 bunch of purple or green seedless grapes, crushed

Cut the cabbage into long, thin strips. Sprinkle salt throughout cabbage, and set aside in a warm place. While cabbage sits, fry diced bacon. Do not discard bacon fat, and add vinegar and grapes. Bring this mixture to a boil. Pour boiling mixture over cabbage and serve. Serves 6.

Old Economy Village

Lemon Cheese Spread

¹/₂ gallon whole milk
2 large lemons
¹/₄ teaspoon salt

This is a simple cheese that can be used as a spread. In a double boiler, warm the milk to 165 degrees, stirring often. Add the juice of 2 lemons to the milk and stir. Take the milk off the stove and allow it to set for 15 minutes. The warm milk will separate into greenish whey. Pour the curds and whey into a cheesecloth-lined colander. Tie the four corners of the cheesecloth into a knot, and allow the curds to drain for an hour, or until they stop dripping. Remove the cheese from the cloth and place into a bowl. Add salt to taste. The cheese will keep for 1 week in the refrigerator. Makes 8 to 10 servings.

Old Economy Village

Left: *Landis Valley Museum.* CRAIG A. BENNER

Granny Smith Apple Chutney

3 pounds (about 9) tart Granny Smith apples; peeled, cored, and diced
2 large onions, chopped
³/₄ cup packed brown sugar
¹/₂ cup golden raisins
1¹/₄ cups cider vinegar
zest of 1 orange, julienned
1 cinnamon stick
¹/₂ teaspoon each salt and ground cloves
¹/₂ cup chopped walnuts, toasted (optional)

Place all ingredients except the nuts in a large saucepan. Bring to a gentle boil and cook uncovered, stirring occasionally, for about 45 minutes or until thickened. If desired, stir in the nuts the last few minutes of cooking. Ladle into hot, sterilized jars, seal, and refrigerate. Keeps for 6 to 8 weeks. Makes about 5 cups. Serve as a condiment with meat dishes or chicken.

Joseph Priestley House

The back kitchen with indoor well at the Joseph Priestley House. Back kitchens were used for preparing food, butchering and drying meat, brewing, and other household tasks. KYLE R. WEAVER

Stuffed Celery

1 celery rib
1¹/₂ ounces Roquefort or bleu cheese
1 ounce butter, softened
¹/₂ teaspoon Angostura Bitters
1¹/₂ tablespoons unsalted almonds, finely chopped

Wash the celery rib well, trim ends, and cut crosswise into 6 pieces. Blend cheese, butter, and bitters together until smooth. Using a small butter knife, fill each piece of celery with a generous mound of the mixture, and while it is still soft, roll in almonds to coat. Place in the refrigerator until very cold, at least 1 hour. Makes 2 servings. *Note:* A popular item on the Pennsylvania Railroad.

Railroad Museum of Pennsylvania

Dandelion Salad with Cooked Dressing

2 cups chopped new dandelion leaves

2 tablespoons chopped onion

4 strips of bacon, fried and cut in small pieces

¹/₄ cup butter

¹/₂ cup cream or milk

I raw egg, beaten

¹/₂ teaspoon salt

dash of pepper

¹/₄ cup cider vinegar

2 tablespoons sugar

I tablespoon flour

2 hard-boiled eggs, sliced or chopped

Toss together chopped dandelion, chopped onion, and fried bacon pieces. Set aside. In skillet, warm butter and cream until butter is melted. Beat raw egg, and then add salt, pepper, vinegar, sugar, and flour. Blend the egg mixture into the slightly warm cream mixture. Increase heat and cook, stirring constantly, until the mixture thickens. Pour hot dressing over the greens and toss gently. Add hard-boiled eggs before tossing. Serve at once. Makes 4 to 6 servings. *Note:* Gather the dandelion leaves early in the spring before the plants flower, or they will be bitter.

Drake Well Museum

Onion Skin–Dyed Easter Eggs

I quart firmly packed onion skins
  (see note below)

2 quarts water

I dozen eggs

I tablespoon apple cider vinegar (optional)

Cover onion skins with water and vinegar and bring to a boil. Simmer about 20 minutes. Remove onion skins and allow the dye bath to cool a little before adding the eggs. Boil about 20 minutes until the eggs are hard-boiled. Refrigerate and use like any other dyed Easter egg. You can dye more eggs in the same bath, but each batch will be lighter in color. *Note:* The type of pot used will alter the color, as does the addition of vinegar. Iron pots will dye eggs a very dark brown, brass pots will give a reddish brown color. Onion skins are the brown, papery outer covering of the onion. Either brown or red onion skins can be used. White onion skins produce no color.

Landis Valley Museum

AN EIGHTEENTH-CENTURY HARVEST DINNER

Graeme Park in Horsham, Montgomery County, reflects the significant influence of the British Isles on many eighteenth-century kitchens in Pennsylvania. That influence was also seen in many of the foods served at Graeme Park in the 1700s. Trade goods and seafood from Philadelphia were complemented by the foodstuffs acquired or grown at Graeme Park and its environs. This duality is also reflected in the following menu for a harvest dinner that was collected from local Bucks County records.

Pumpkin soup

Roast turkey or wild goose with cornbread, sausage, and apple stuffing

Fricassee of rabbit

Scalloped oysters

Corn pudding

Sweet potatoes with apples and nuts

Cranberry chutney

Creamed onions

Bread and butter

Apple, mince, and pumpkin pies

Raspberry fool

Cider, rum, beer, and wine

At work in the summer kitchen at Graeme Park. KYLE R. WEAVER

Pickled Red Beets

6 to 8 medium red beets
2 cups sugar
1 1/2 cups raspberry-flavored wine vinegar
1/2 cup water
salt and pepper to taste

Wash beets and remove all but 1 inch of the stems. Boil in water until soft. Cool until they can be handled comfortably. Remove outer skins and cut into slices. Place in a large bowl or crock. In a medium saucepan, bring the sugar, vinegar, and water to a boil. Cook only until sugar is dissolved. Add salt and pepper. You can add onions, coriander seeds, cloves, or horseradish if desired. Cool. Refrigerate at least 8 to 10 hours before serving. Makes 6 to 8 servings. *Note:* The Pennsylvania Dutch dialect term *riewe* is applied to carrots, red beets, and all turnips. That's why the Pennsylvania Dutchman specifically says red beets rather than just beets.

Landis Valley Museum

Red Beet Eggs

Hard-boil 12 to 18 eggs. Cool and remove from shell. Put into large jar or crock. Cover with pickled red beet slices (above). Add liquid from beets last, using enough to cover eggs with liquid. Refrigerate at least 24 to 48 hours before using. *Note:* This is a traditional Pennsylvania Dutch food served at holidays and picnics. They are especially pretty halved or sliced and served in a nice dish with the sliced red beets.

Landis Valley Museum

Cranberry Chutney

1 pound cranberries
1 tart apple; pared, cored, and diced
2 cups brown sugar
3/4 cup vinegar
1/2 cup chopped mixed candied fruit and peels
1/2 teaspoon salt
1/4 teaspoon each dried mustard, ground ginger, cloves, and allspice

Combine all ingredients in a 3-quart pan and bring to a boil. Reduce heat and simmer uncovered for 15 minutes, stirring occasionally. Cool and refrigerate in an airtight container. Makes 4 1/2 cups. An excellent condiment with chicken or turkey.

Graeme Park

PENNSYLVANIA STATE ARCHIVES

Bread and Butter Pickles

4 quarts small to medium cucumbers

6 medium white onions, sliced

2 green peppers, chopped

3 cloves garlic, peeled

¹/₃ cup pickling salt

cracked ice

5 cups sugar

3 cups cider vinegar

1¹/₂ teaspoons turmeric

1¹/₂ teaspoons celery seed

2 tablespoons mustard seed

Don't pare cucumbers, but be sure there is no wax or oil on them. Slice thin. Add onions, peppers, whole garlic cloves, and salt. Cover with cracked ice. Mix well and allow to stand 3 hours. Drain well. Combine remaining ingredients. Pour over cucumbers. Heat just to a boil. Seal in hot, sterilized jars. Makes 8 pints.

Landis Valley Museum

Scotch Eggs

Lay several fresh eggs in warm ashes. (*Caution:* Keep eggs away from red coals, or they may explode.) Using tongs, turn eggs several times. In about 1 1/4 to 1 1/2 hours, the eggs will be hard-cooked. When cool enough to handle, peel eggs. Cover them with a layer of forcemeat (forcemeat is usually veal, but seasoned sausage is good in this recipe). Place meat-covered eggs in a skillet over medium heat. Cook until all meat is done, then remove eggs to platter. Cut eggs in half lengthwise. Pour beef broth around eggs, but not over them. Serve immediately.

Graeme Park

Boiled Bacon Dressing

4 or 5 strips of bacon, diced

2 eggs

1/2 cup sugar

1 tablespoon flour

1/4 cup vinegar

3/4 cup water

Fry diced bacon. Beat eggs, sugar, and flour together. Add vinegar and then water and stir well. Add mixture to bacon and bring to a boil. Pour over dandelion, lettuce, or endive that has been washed and drained. Serve immediately. Makes 4 to 6 servings.

Cornwall Iron Furnace

Sausage Biscuits

2 cups flour

1 teaspoon salt

2 1/2 teaspoons baking powder

1/4 cup shortening

1/2 cup milk

1 1/2 pounds pork or venison sausage (loose, not links)

Sift flour once, then measure. Add salt and baking powder; sift into mixing bowl. Cut in shortening with two knives until the mixture resembles coarse meal. Add milk; stir with fork until soft dough is formed. Turn out on a lightly floured surface; knead 15 to 20 times. Roll pieces of dough 1/4 inch thick and 3 to 4 inches in diameter. Shape sausage into balls the size of an English walnut. Wrap dough around sausage until sealed. Place in greased pan. Bake in a preheated 375-degree oven for 25 to 30 minutes, or until brown. Makes about 20 biscuits.

Daniel Boone Homestead

Soups

Salsify or Vegetable Oyster Soup

1 ¹/₂ cups diced salsify root

1 ¹/₂ cups water

1 tablespoon vinegar

1 tablespoon butter

1 quart milk

salt and pepper to taste

Scrub, scrape, and clean salsify root. Dice and cook in salted water with vinegar added until tender. Drain. Add butter, milk, salt, and pepper. Bring to a boil. Serve with crackers. Makes 4 servings. *Note:* Salsify is often referred to as "vegetable oyster" because the root has an oyster-like taste.

Joseph Priestley House

Corn Chowder

4 cups potatoes, peeled and diced

2 cups water

2 tablespoons salt pork, diced

3 tablespoons onion, chopped

2 cups corn kernels, fresh or canned

2 cups milk

2 teaspoons salt

¹/₂ teaspoon pepper

Cook potatoes in water for 15 minutes. In skillet, cook salt pork and onions until browned; add corn, milk, and seasonings to potatoes and water. Heat, but do not boil. Makes 6 servings.

Museum of Anthracite Mining

Left: *Bushy Run Battlefield.* ART BECKER

Fruktsoppa (Swedish Fruit Soup)

³/₄ cup dried apricots

³/₄ cup dried prunes

6 cups water

I cinnamon stick

2 slices of lemon, ¹/₄ inch thick

3 tablespoons quick-cooking tapioca

I cup sugar

2 tablespoons raisins

I tablespoon dried currants

I tart cooking apple, peeled, cored, and cut into ¹/₂-inch slices

Soak the dried apricots and prunes in 6 cups cold water for 30 minutes. Since the dried fruit expands as it absorbs the water, you will need at least a 3-quart stainless steel or enameled saucepan. Add the cinnamon stick, lemon slices, tapioca, and sugar. Bring to a boil, then reduce heat, cover, and simmer for 10 minutes, stirring occasionally with a wooden spoon to prevent sticking. Stir in the raisins, currants, and apple slices. Simmer an additional 5 minutes, or until the apples are tender. Pour the soup into a large serving bowl and let cool to room temperature. Remove the cinnamon stick. Cover and refrigerate to chill. Makes 6 servings.

Morton Homestead

Pork and Chicken Soup

4- to 5-pound stewing chicken

¹/₂ pound slab bacon (or extra-thick sliced bacon)

3 onions, finely chopped

2 or 3 small carrots, finely diced

2 cups brown or white rice

salt and pepper to taste

Wash the chicken well and remove excess fat. Put in a large kettle, cover with water, and bring to a boil. Boil until tender. Meanwhile, cut the bacon into small cubes, and fry until crisp and brown. Drain bacon, reserving the grease. Chop the onions fine, and fry in the bacon grease. Drain and set aside. Remove the chicken from the broth and allow to cool. Discard the skin and cut the meat into bite-size pieces. Set aside. Finely dice the carrots and add to the chicken broth. Add the rice, and cook until the rice is tender, following the package directions. Usually white rice takes about 20 minutes, and brown rice takes about 45 minutes to cook. About 10 minutes before rice is done, add the chicken, bacon, and onions. Add salt and pepper to taste. Makes 4 to 6 servings.

Landis Valley Museum

Chicken Creole Soup

I onion, diced

2 green peppers, finely chopped

2 15-ounce cans crushed tomatoes

2 quarts chicken stock

I whole pimiento, julienned

I cup cooked rice

I cup cooked chicken, finely diced

$^{1}/_{2}$ cup flour

salt and pepper to taste

In 4-quart saucepan, combine onion, peppers, tomatoes, and chicken stock. Bring to a boil, reduce heat, and simmer for 30 minutes. Then add pimiento, rice, and chicken, and heat through. Add flour, stirring constantly to thicken. Season with salt and pepper. The finished soup will be a creamy pink color, with red pimientos and green peppers floating on top. Makes 8 servings. *Note:* This was a popular soup on the Reading Railroad.

Railroad Museum of Pennsylvania

Railcar designs for the Pennsylvania Railroad, 1938–39, by Raymond Loewy. DON GILES/ RAILROAD MUSEUM OF PENNSYLVANIA

Native American Butternut Squash Soup

2 large butternut squashes
salt to taste
honey to taste
¹/₄ cup pumpkin seeds
chopped chives

Skin the squashes and cut into 2-inch pieces. Place in heavy saucepan, cover with water, and cook over medium heat until fork-tender. Drain and reserve liquid. Put squash in food processor and process until smooth, adding reserved liquid as needed if too thick. Add salt and honey to taste. Place pumpkin seeds on baking sheet, and roast at 350 degrees. Ladle soup into bowls, and garnish with chives and pumpkin seeds. Makes 6 servings.

Conrad Weiser Homestead

Colonial Philadelphia Black Bean Soup

2 cups dried black beans
2 quarts water
2 medium onions, chopped
3 celery ribs, chopped
¹/₈ teaspoon thyme
¹/₈ teaspoon allspice
I small bay leaf
I teaspoon ground mustard seed
4 whole cloves
I tablespoon Worcestershire sauce
I ham hock
¹/₄ cup sherry
2 hard-boiled eggs, sliced
I lemon

Soak the beans in cold water to cover overnight. Drain well and add the 2 quarts water, vegetables, seasonings, and ham hock. Bring to a boil and cook over low heat for 2 hours, or until beans are tender. Remove ham and cut in small pieces; set aside. Puree soup in a blender or food processor, and return to pot. Add sherry and meat. Taste and adjust seasonings, if necessary. If too thick, add more water. Serve in bowl with a slice of egg atop a slice of lemon floating on the surface. Makes 6 to 8 servings.

Hope Lodge

CRAIG A. BENNER

Pumpkin Soup Baked in Its Shell

1 medium pumpkin (about 8 inches in diameter)

3 to 4 cups milk or light cream

3 tablespoons butter

1 medium onion, finely chopped

3 tablespoons honey, brown sugar, or maple syrup

pinch of salt

1 teaspoon nutmeg (or to taste)

Cut off top of pumpkin and take out seeds and membranes. Fill cavity halfway with milk or light cream. Add the rest of the ingredients. Replace top and place pumpkin in baking dish with about 1 inch of water. Bake at 350 degrees for 1 1/2 hours. Test for softness before removing. Before serving, scrape the cooked flesh out of the pumpkin into the milk mixture, mixing thoroughly. Place entire pumpkin on serving dish and take to the table for a great presentation. Ladle soup into bowls, and season with additional butter, salt, and nutmeg to taste. Makes 6 to 8 servings.

Brandywine Battlefield Park

PITHOLE OYSTERS

Like chicken wings today, in the nineteenth century, oysters were wildly popular. Oysters were cheap and plentiful, and every town in areas where they could be shipped inland had oyster parlors, oyster cellars, oyster saloons, oyster bars, oyster houses, oyster stalls, and oyster lunchrooms. The primary source of oysters in nineteenth-century Pennsylvania was the Chesapeake Bay, which produced 10,000,000 to 14,000,000 tons annually. There was even a recipe for mock oyster soup, made from salsify (page 9), when the real thing was not available.

Former Civil War soldiers, who acquired a taste for canned oysters during their military service, created a demand for this delicacy in the booming oil fields of Pennsylvania. Oil wealth meant they could afford the luxury of the fresh oysters that traveled by train from Baltimore to Titusville packed in barrels of sawdust and ice. Despite the long trip from the Chesapeake and the fifteen-mile wagon trip over steep hills and heavily rutted muddy roads to Pithole, most of the oysters seem to have arrived in edible condition. Those who stepped up to the marble counters of the oyster bars consumed the raw oysters as fast as the shuckers could ready them, without bothering with a plate. Local lore was that the consumption of alcoholic beverages with the oysters killed any bacteria that might have poisoned diners.

At one time, Pennsylvania led the world in oil production. Pennsylvania's historic oil industry is chronicled at Drake Well Museum and Park in Venango County and at the site of nearby Pithole City.

Pennsylvania's oil boom began in Titusville on August 27, 1859, when Edwin L. Drake perfected a way to drill for oil and extract it from the ground. In 1865, oil was discovered at Pithole, and by September of the same year, Pithole had grown from a farming area to a city of 15,000, complete with restaurants, fifty hotels, theaters, saloons, dance halls, and even brothels. But Pithole declined almost as rapidly as it grew. The supply of oil petered out, the population shrank (by the end of 1866, it had dwindled to less than 2,000), and the hastily constructed wooden buildings gradually disappeared. Today nothing remains of this boomtown but cellar holes in a hillside meadow.

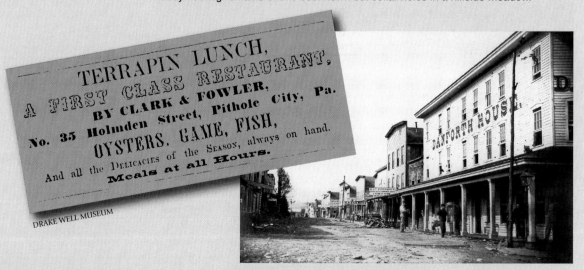

TERRAPIN LUNCH,
A FIRST CLASS RESTAURANT,
BY CLARK & FOWLER,
No. 35 Holmden Street, Pithole City, Pa.
OYSTERS, GAME, FISH,
And all the DELICACIES of the SEASON, always on hand.
Meals at all Hours.

DRAKE WELL MUSEUM

Pithole City, where countless oysters were consumed during the oil boom. DRAKE WELL MUSEUM

Oyster Stew

2 quarts oysters and liquor
8 cups milk, scalded
4 tablespoons butter
salt and pepper to taste

Heat oysters in their liquor about 5 minutes, until the edges curl. Skim off the top. Combine oysters and liquor with the scalded milk. Add butter, and season to taste. Serve immediately. Makes 4 servings.

Drake Well Museum

Chicken Corn Soup

1 4-pound stewing chicken
1 cup chopped onion
1 tablespoon salt
1/4 teaspoon pepper
1 cup chopped celery with leaves
2 10-ounce packages frozen corn
1 cup sifted flour
1/2 teaspoon salt
1 raw egg
1 to 2 tablespoons milk
2 hard-boiled eggs, chopped

About five hours before serving, place chicken, onion, salt, and pepper in a large kettle. Add water to cover. Simmer, covered, about 2$1/2$ hours, or until chicken is almost tender. Remove chicken from broth; discard skin and bones, and cut meat into bite-size pieces. Return chicken to broth along with celery and corn. Continue simmering, covered, about 20 minutes. Meanwhile, prepare rivels. In a bowl, combine flour, salt, raw egg, and milk—enough to make a crumblike mixture. From spoon, drop rivels and chopped hard-boiled eggs into simmering soup. Cook uncovered about 20 minutes, or until rivels are tender. Season with salt and pepper to taste. Makes 10 generous servings.

Cornwall Iron Furnace

The hearth at Conrad Weiser Homestead. KYLE R. WEAVER

Corn Soup

9 ears sweet green corn
water or veal or chicken stock
onion, chopped
salt and pepper to taste
1 cup heavy cream
flour

Scrape off all the kernels from the ears of corn. Put the cobs in sufficient water or stock to make a tureen of soup, boil until all the sweet juice is extracted, then throw away the cobs. Season the broth with salt, pepper, and a little chopped onion. Add the corn kernels, and boil them just long enough to become tender. Slowly stir in cream, thickened with a very little flour. Makes 8 servings. *Note:* This soup is much better with veal or chicken stock instead of water.

Cornwall Iron Furnace

Acorn Squash Soup

4 acorn squashes

3 carrots, sliced

I onion, sliced

¹/₃ cup water

2 tablespoons butter

I tablespoon flour

I teaspoon salt

¹/₂ to I teaspoon pepper

29 ounces chicken broth

¹/₂ cup sherry

¹/₂ teaspoon ground nutmeg

¹/₈ teaspoon paprika

dash ground allspice

dash red pepper

I cup half-and-half

I ¹/₂ tablespoons sherry (optional)

paprika (for garnish)

Cut squash in half lengthwise and remove seeds. Place squash halves, cut side down, in a broiler pan. Add hot water to a depth of 1 inch. Bake at 350 degrees for 30 minutes. Spoon pulp from squash halves to create serving bowls, reserving pulp. Place carrots and onion in a saucepan; cover with water. Bring to a boil, then cover, reduce heat, and simmer for 15 minutes, or until vegetables are tender. Drain; combine vegetables with reserved pulp and ¹/₃ cup water in blender or food processor. Process for 30 seconds, or until mixture is smooth. Set aside. Melt butter in a large Dutch oven over low heat; add flour, salt, and pepper, stirring until smooth. Cook for 1 minute, stirring constantly. Gradually add pureed vegetable mixture, chicken broth, sherry, nutmeg, paprika, allspice, and red pepper; bring to a boil. Cover, reduce heat, and simmer for 1 hour, stirring occasionally. Stir in half-and-half and, if desired, sherry. Cook until heated. Spoon into squash bowls and sprinkle with paprika. Makes 8 servings.

Conrad Weiser Homestead

Breads

Potato Scones

¹/₂ pound potatoes, boiled and peeled
I tablespoon butter
¹/₂ cup flour
pinch salt

Mash potatoes smoothly, adding dots of butter and pinch of salt. Beat well. Gradually work in as much flour as potatoes will absorb. Turn onto a floured board and roll out thin. Cut into bannocks (large circles) and then into quarters. Prick all over with a fork. Bake on griddle for about 5 minutes, turning once. Cool scones on towel, butter them at once, roll up, and serve hot. They should be eaten the day they are made and are good with butter and honey, syrup, or jam. Makes 8 to 10 scones.

Graeme Park

Sweet Scones

3 cups flour
2 tablespoons baking powder
I cup sugar
I cup butter
I egg, beaten, with enough milk to make I cup
I cup dried cranberries, currants, raisins, or other fruits

Mix together dry ingredients. Cut in butter, then add liquids and fruit. Drop on ovenproof griddle by the spoonful, or roll out and place on griddle. Bake in 425- to 450-degree oven for 5 minutes, turn, and bake 5 minutes more. Makes 2 dozen scones.

Daniel Boone Homestead

Left: *Somerset Historical Center.* TERRY WAY/COMMONWEALTH MEDIA SERVICES

THE LOVE FEAST

Founded in 1732 by Conrad Beissel along the Cocalico Creek in Lancaster County, Ephrata Cloister was one of America's earliest religious communities. Although some members were celibate, there were married members who lived in individual homes, had children, cultivated farms, and were similar to their Pennsylvania Dutch neighbors.

Many members of the Ephrata community led a strictly disciplined lifestyle in the hope that their souls would unite with God. Daily life at Ephrata stressed the ascetic life, with a monastic schedule and dress. Members spent only six hours at rest each day, divided by a two-hour midnight worship service, and tried to subsist with little daily nourishment. Believing that certain foods aroused distracting ideas, members generally avoided meat. A 1753 account describes an evening meal consisting of pearled barley boiled in milk with bread broken into it, pumpkin mush, and slices of bread with butter.

The most important ritual celebrated at Ephrata was the Love Feast, which was held periodically within the community. The ritual could last five to six hours and included three parts: foot washing, a fellowship meal, and holy communion. Foot washing symbolized humility and a possible cleansing from sin, and in Ephrata was also a sign of hospitality.

The communal meal was more ample than the ordinarily spare meals. The usual ban on meat was relaxed for the occasion, and lamb stew was often served—a reminder of Christ as the Lamb of God and Shepherd of the flock. Love Feasts were held on a number of occasions, including building dedications and memorials for members who had died. They could involve the whole community or just select individuals.

In western Pennsylvania, another community practiced the Love Feast *(Liebesmahl):* the Harmony Society at Old Economy Village in Ambridge, Beaver County. Founded in Germany in 1785, the Harmony Society ultimately moved to Economy in 1825 under the leadership of George Rapp (1757–1847). Members signed a covenant turning over all

A dining area in the Saron at Ephrata Cloister. CRAIG A. BENNER

their possessions to the society, which then agreed to supply all necessities. Celibacy was strictly adhered to, and husbands and wives were expected to live as though they were brother and sister. The community supported itself as a manufacturing organization, primarily through wool, silk, and textile production.

The Love Feast was held in the Feast Hall and Museum Building (1826), the largest building of the Harmonist complex. Because outsiders were not invited to their Love Feasts, little is known about the meals. They probably included a stew of beef, pork, or lamb, along with rice or spaetzel. Before the feast, members confessed all their individual differences before Father Rapp and might have participated in the ritual of giving each other the "kiss of peace" on the cheek.

Love Feasts were held on the anniversary of the society's founding (February 15), on Easter, Christmas, Harvest Home, and often when there was a perceived need. When there was a schism within the group in 1832, Love Feasts were held as often as three times a week in an effort to resolve divisive problems. The meal and religious service of each feast lasted all day.

The Feast Hall at Old Economy Village. ART BECKER

Onion Dumplings

¹/₃ **cup minced onions**
1 to 1¹/₂ tablespoons bacon fat (or butter)
1 tablespoon butter
¹/₂ **cup flour**
¹/₄ **teaspoon salt**
¹/₈ **teaspoon grated nutmeg**
2 eggs
about ¹/₄ cup heavy cream
5 to 6 cups water
1 tablespoon salt
melted butter for serving

Brown onions in bacon fat or butter. In mixing bowl, cream 1 tablespoon butter, then mix in flour, salt, nutmeg, onions, and eggs. Add cream till the batter is a thick consistency and not sticky. Roll batter into balls by rounded tablespoonfuls, and drop into boiling salted water. Do not allow dumplings to stick to bottom. Continue boiling until dumplings float to the top, about 2 to 4 minutes. Serve with melted butter. Makes about 1 dozen dumplings.

Old Economy Village

Miniature Potato Knishes

1 medium onion, diced
3 cups mashed potatoes
2 large eggs, lightly beaten
2 tablespoons margarine
1 teaspoon salt
$^1/_8$ teaspoon pepper
$^3/_8$ cup matzo meal
vegetable cooking spray
1 large egg yolk, beaten with 1 tablespoon water

Sauté onion until browned. In bowl, combine mashed potatoes with eggs, margarine, salt, pepper, and matzo meal. Add sautéed onion. Form into walnut-size balls. Place on cookie sheets that have been sprayed with cooking spray. Brush with diluted egg yolk. Bake for 20 minutes in a 400-degree oven or until browned. Makes 36 knishes.

The State Museum of Pennsylvania

Wigs

1 package dry yeast
$^1/_4$ cup warm water
1$^1/_2$ cups warm milk
6 cups flour
1$^1/_2$ teaspoons salt
1 egg, beaten
$^3/_4$ cup sugar
$^1/_2$ cup butter, softened
1 tablespoon caraway seeds
$^1/_4$ teaspoon nutmeg
pinch ground cloves
pinch mace

Add yeast to warm water. When dissolved, add milk. Sift flour and salt into liquid, and stir until blended. Mix in egg, sugar, butter, seeds, and spices. Cover bowl, put in warm place free from drafts, and let double in bulk. Stir down and add enough flour to make a kneadable dough. Turn out onto floured board, and knead for about 5 minutes. Place in a greased bowl, cover, and let double in bulk again. Punch down and turn out onto floured board. Roll out to $^1/_4$ to $^1/_2$ inch thickness. Cut into wedges or whatever shape is desired. Place on greased baking sheets. Bake at 375 degrees for about 20 minutes, or until lightly browned. Makes 24 to 48 buns, depending on size and thickness.

Hope Lodge

Diamond Cheese Biscuits

1/4 **pound lard, softened**
1/4 **pound butter, softened**
8 cups sifted flour
1 tablespoon salt
2 tablespoons sugar
2 tablespoons baking powder
1/2 **pound American cheese, grated**
2 1/2 **cups milk**
yolk of 1 egg
1 tablespoon light cream

In a large mixing bowl, use a pastry cutter to work lard and butter into flour until coarse. Add salt, sugar, baking powder, and cheese, and mix thoroughly. Slowly add milk, stirring until mixture is of biscuit-dough consistency. On a lightly floured surface, roll dough out to 3/4 inch thickness. Use a sharp knife to cut dough into 2x3-inch diamond shapes. Place biscuits on greased baking sheet. Make an egg wash by beating egg yolk and cream together lightly. Brush wash atop biscuits, and bake until lightly browned, about 25 minutes. Makes 36 biscuits. *Note:* This was popular fare on the Reading Railroad.

Railroad Museum of Pennsylvania

Sally Lunn Bread

2 packages dry yeast
1/4 **cup lukewarm water**
1 cup milk
1/4 **cup soft butter**
3 1/2 **cups flour**
1 teaspoon salt
2 eggs

Dissolve yeast in lukewarm water, and set aside. Heat milk and butter until warm, and combine with dissolved yeast. Sift 1 1/2 cups of the flour with salt into a large bowl. Gradually add liquid, beating until smooth. Beat eggs until light. Stir into batter until thoroughly blended. Gradually add remaining flour, beating until smooth. Cover bowl and let batter rise in warm place until doubled in bulk. Stir batter down. Pour into well-greased tube or bundt pan. Cover and let batter rise again until doubled. Bake 30 to 40 minutes, until done. Makes 1 loaf.

Hope Lodge

LUMBER CAMPS AND LUMBERJACKS

One of the most interesting attractions at the Pennsylvania Lumber Museum in Galeton, Potter County, is the mess hall, which depicts one aspect of the life of lumberjacks in the heyday of Pennsylvania's nineteenth-century lumber camps.

When William Penn arrived in 1682, it is estimated that 90 percent of the state's 20,000,000 acres was covered with dense stands of white pine, eastern hemlock, and mixed hardwoods. When Pennsylvania's lumber industry peaked between 1850 and 1870, the state was the world's largest producer of lumber. Wood was needed for new homes and businesses, ships, firewood to heat homes, and charcoal for iron furnaces. To meet the demand for wood, loggers wielded handheld axes and two-man crosscut saws.

Lumberjacks had to be well fed, consuming an average of 8,000 calories a day to provide the

Left: *A lumber camp mess hall, late nineteenth century.* PENNSYLVANIA STATE ARCHIVES

Below: *The mess hall re-creation at Pennsylvania Lumber Museum.* COMMONWEALTH MEDIA SERVICES

energy needed to tackle the rigors of hard physical labor, especially during the cold winter months when much of the logging took place. One sound not heard during meals, often only five minutes long, was that of voices. Talking was forbidden at meals, as conversation among such a diverse group of men, living and working in close quarters, often led to fights.

Feeding a large crew of hungry loggers—as many as 75 to 100 in each camp—was quite a challenge for the lumber company cook and his assistants. Breakfast might include eggs, bacon, sausage, pancakes (below), and coffee or tea. Lunch pails were taken by sled or handcar to the lumberjacks so that they could remain close to the work area and finish quickly.

A hearty dinner generally featured meats, potatoes, Lumber Camp Skillet (page 36), vegetables, breads, and desserts. Loggers coined nicknames for food, including cackleberries (eggs), stovelids (pancakes), doorknobs (biscuits), goldfish (canned salmon), gravel (salt), sand (sugar), redlead (ketchup), logging berries (prunes), Murphys (potatoes), slush or blackjack (coffee), and swamp water (tea).

Logging railroads brought lumberjacks into previously inaccessible areas. PENNSYLVANIA STATE ARCHIVES

Lumberjack Pancakes

2 cups buttermilk

2 eggs

2 teaspoons baking soda

¹/₄ teaspoon salt

1 teaspoon oil

¹/₄ cup toasted wheat germ

1 ¹/₂ to 2 cups flour

Using a wire whisk, mix together buttermilk, eggs, and baking soda. Add salt, oil, and wheat germ. Mix in flour to thicken. For thinner pancakes, add more buttermilk. Makes 3 to 6 pancakes. *Note:* Lumberjacks consumed eight to twelve thousand calories a day. These pancakes were only part of their breakfast, which might also include eggs, meat, potatoes, biscuits, and doughnuts.

Pennsylvania Lumber Museum

Pierogi (Polish)

Dough

3 1/4 cups flour
1 egg
1/2 cup water
dash salt

Filling

1 pound farmers cheese
1 egg yolk
dash salt

Mix the egg into the flour; add salt and as much water as needed to form a soft, pliable dough. Roll dough out very thinly and cut into 3-inch squares. Mix together filling ingredients. Place about 1 teaspoon filling on each square, then fold the dough over the filling to make a triangle. Pinch edges together. Cook for 5 minutes in boiling salted water. Remove and drain. Serve with 1 large onion, chopped and sautéed in 1/4 cup butter. Makes 4 to 6 servings.

Anthracite Heritage Museum
Eckley Miners' Village

Cottage Cheese Dumplings

1 1/2 cups butter
3 eggs
6 generous tablespoons cottage cheese
1/2 teaspoon nutmeg
2 tablespoons sugar
1/2 teaspoon salt
about 1 1/2 cups bread crumbs
milk (optional)
flour
5 to 6 cups water
1 teaspoon salt

Squeeze out cottage cheese, using cheesecloth. Cream butter, then add eggs and cheese. Fold in nutmeg, sugar, 1/2 teaspoon salt, and bread crumbs. You may need more or less bread crumbs, depending on the dough consistency. Thin with milk if necessary. Dust hands with flour, and shape the dough into rough dumplings. Cook dumplings in water with 1 teaspoon salt. Done when dumplings float or when a knife inserted in center comes out clean. Good served with brown sugar, maple syrup, apple butter, or applesauce. Makes 6 servings.

Old Economy Village

Slices: The Poor Knights

¹/₂ cup flour

¹/₄ cup sugar

2 eggs

pinch salt

²/₃ cup milk

home-baked-style bread

additional milk for soaking bread

butter

sugar and cinnamon for dusting

Whisk flour, sugar, eggs, salt, and milk into a thin batter. Slice bread into ¹/₂-inch slices, and moisten in milk. Dip the moistened slices into batter. Lay the slices on a baking sheet that has been well greased with butter. Bake for 12 to 15 minutes at 400 degrees, until slices are firm. After baking, dust with sugar and cinnamon. Makes 6 servings.

Old Economy Village

Italian Easter Pitz (Pizza)

4 cups flour

I teaspoon salt

I egg

I cup shortening

I ¹/₄ cups water

Combine dry ingredients. Cut in shortening, and then add egg. Add water until it forms dough. Roll out dough mixture and place in a 13x9-inch pan (preferably glass).

Topping

I pound sausage (half hot, half mild), cooked and diced

I pound boneless smoked ham

I pound ricotta cheese

6 boiled eggs, diced

I dozen raw eggs

¹/₂ cup Romano cheese

parsley

Mix all together and pour onto crust in baking pan. Bake at 375 degrees about 1 hour. Take out of pan and cool on brown paper. Cut into squares. Store in brown paper bag in refrigerator. Makes 6 to 8 servings.

Anthracite Heritage Museum
Eckley Miners' Village

Hardtack

I cup unbleached flour
I teaspoon salt
$^1/_2$ cup warm water

Scoop flour into mixing bowl. Add salt, then warm water—a little at a time. Knead the dough as you add the water. It should not be sticky or very dry. Once the dough is of the right consistency, roll it out flat to about $^3/_8$ inch thickness. Cut into 3x3-inch to 4x4-inch squares. (The regulation-size hardtack was about $3^1/_2$ inches.) Using a small wooden dowel, punch about 16 holes into each square. Place the squares onto a baking sheet, and bake at 400 degrees until just turning golden brown. Reduce the oven temperature to 200 degrees, and bake for 2 more hours. Then turn the oven off and let the hardtack cool in the oven overnight. It's important that as much moisture as possible is baked out of the hardtack. If not, it will get moldy. Stored in a dry environment, it should last several months. Nothing else should be added to the hardtack—no raisins, cinnamon, or yeast. Hardtack by itself is pretty hard and tasteless. Period accounts state that often the soldiers soaked the hardtack in cold water, and then fried it up in bacon fat. It can also be broken up and added to stew as a substitute for dumplings. Makes about 10 pieces.

Erie Maritime Museum and U.S. Brig Niagara,
Brandywine Battlefield Park

Holiday Ricotta Cheese Bread

$3^1/_2$ to 4 cups flour
I package dry yeast
I teaspoon sugar
$^1/_4$ cup very warm water
$^3/_4$ cup milk, heated to boiling
2 tablespoons butter
I teaspoon salt
I large egg

Combine all ingredients and beat with electric mixer about 5 minutes, or until smooth. Let rise in greased bowl until double in bulk. Knead by hand if you do not have a dough hook. Divide into thirds and roll out on floured board into sheets 8 inches in diameter and 1 inch thick.

Filling

2 cups ricotta cheese
$^1/_2$ teaspoon salt

AT SEA YESTERDAY AND TODAY

The Erie Maritime Museum, in Erie, serves as the home port of the U.S. Brig *Niagara*, a historically accurate reconstruction of Oliver Hazard Perry's relief flagship from the Battle of Lake Erie in the War of 1812.

On September 10, 1813, Perry engaged the British at the Battle of Lake Erie near Put-in-Bay, Ohio. When his flagship, the *Lawrence,* was seriously damaged during the battle, Perry took command of the Brig *Niagara*. With a fresh crew and quickening wind, the *Niagara* closed in and inflicted the finishing blows on the British flagships, the *Queen Charlotte* and the *Detroit*. The British surrendered on the deck of the *Lawrence,* and Perry penned his famous message, "We have met the enemy and they are ours."

Hardtack. ERIE MARITIME MUSEUM

With the Great Lakes secured, in 1820 the *Lawrence* and the *Niagara* were scuttled in Misery Bay near Erie. In 1875, the remains of the *Lawrence* were raised and taken to Philadelphia to be displayed at the Centennial, but while awaiting exhibition, the vestiges of the ship burned in a warehouse fire.

In March 1913, the remains of the *Niagara* were raised for the centennial of the Battle of Lake Erie. Using some of the timbers of the original ship, and without any original plans, a new *Niagara* was built. Over time, this ship decayed, until a reconstruction project was begun in 1931. In 1943, the *Niagara* was launched, but insufficient funding prevented the completion of masts, spars, and sails. Eventually the ship was placed in a concrete cradle on land, but by 1987, it was unsalvageable and was dismantled.

In 1988, construction of a new *Niagara* got under way, supported by the Pennsylvania Historical and Museum Commission, the Commonwealth of Pennsylvania, and the Flagship Niagara League. In 1990, the U.S. Brig *Niagara* was commissioned as the official "Flagship of Pennsylvania."

Today the brig's home port is the Erie Maritime Museum. When the ship is sailing, she carries a crew of 40 men and women, far less than the 155 men who sailed on her in 1813. Rations were meager, including hardtack (page 28) and Johnny cake (page 30), as well as a daily issue of grog—whiskey and water. Today's crew enjoys a more varied menu, with recipes such as U.S. Brig *Niagara* lunch casserole (page 47) and birthday brownies (page 98), but no grog. The professional and volunteer crew, who sleep in hammocks below decks, are fed in the ship's galley, where meals are prepared on a wood stove.

^{1}/$_2$ **cup Romano or Parmesan cheese**

^{1}/$_4$ **stick pepperoni, sliced very thin**

Mix all ingredients together thoroughly with spoon. Spread mixture on center of each dough sheet. Fold dough over mixture, seal edges firmly, and place on greased cookie sheet. Bake about 45 minutes at 400 degrees. Brush with milk 5 minutes before done. Cook until golden brown. Cool, then slice to serve. Makes 16 servings.

Cornwall Iron Furnace

Raised Buckwheat Griddle Cakes

3 cups buckwheat flour

I cup all-purpose, unbleached, or whole wheat flour

I teaspoon salt

4 cups warm water, divided

I package dry yeast

I teaspoon sugar or 1/2 teaspoon honey

2 tablespoons brown sugar or molasses

3/4 teaspoon baking soda

I tablespoon vegetable oil

Combine flours and salt in large bowl—large enough that the flours only fill it halfway, because the batter will expand. Soften yeast in 1/4 cup warm water. Combine sugar or honey with 3 3/4 cups warm water; mix with yeast mixture. Stir into dry ingredients. Cover; let stand overnight at room temperature. The next morning, stir in brown sugar or molasses, soda, and oil. Reserve 1 cup batter for starter for the next batch, storing in refrigerator, where it will keep for several weeks. Spoon remaining batter on a hot, lightly greased griddle. Makes 20 pancakes.

Griddle Cakes from Starter

I cup reserved batter

I cup lukewarm water

1/2 cup buckwheat flour

1/2 cup all-purpose, unbleached, or whole wheat flour

1/2 teaspoon salt

1/2 teaspoon baking soda

2 tablespoons brown sugar or molasses

I tablespoon vegetable oil

Add water and flours to reserved batter and stir well. Let stand overnight. When ready to use, add salt, soda, brown sugar or molasses, and oil. Cook as above, again reserving 1 cup of the batter for the next batch.

Daniel Boone Homestead

Johnny Cake (Journeycake)

I cup flour

I cup yellow cornmeal

3/4 cup brown sugar

I teaspoon salt

I teaspoon baking soda

FEEDING REVOLUTIONARY WAR SOLDIERS

People who visit battlefields and historic encampment sites take for granted the enjoyment of a picnic or dining at a nearby restaurant, but Revolutionary War soldiers had no such luxuries. The Continental Congress on June 16, 1775, authorized appointment of a quartermaster general and a commissary general of stores and provisions for the Continental Army.

Officially, soldiers were to be issued daily rations that were to include meat (often beef or pork), bread (often hardtack), dry beans or peas, and a gill of rum or beer. Salted and dried foods were necessary because there were no other practical means of food preservation. Often soldiers boiled their dried beans or peas with the meat to make a makeshift stew. Many soldiers resorted to soaking their hardtack (page 28) in warm water or stew to soften it. Milk, turnips, potatoes, onions, and fish might also appear on the menu.

While it was the intent of the Continental Congress to provide ample rations for soldiers, good intentions were not enough to keep the army fed. Soldiers were lucky to receive even half their rations, and this did not provide them with a balanced diet. Vegetables were often in short supply. Vinegar was later added to the rations to prevent scurvy, but it often was not available. Transportation of supplies was the most serious problem, not only for the Continental Army, but more significantly for the British Army. Soldiers often relied on local purchases, food donations, and food sent by their families. They also hunted game and gathered wild foods and herbs along the way.

Gen. George Washington authorized local farmers to sell their products at camp markets, but most soldiers had little money to buy food. Justifying their actions by necessity of war, soldiers learned to "liberate" provisions. One sergeant recorded that when his patrol happened upon a sheep and two large turkeys "not being able to give the Countersign," they were "tryd by fire and executed by the whole Division of the free Booters."

For more information about life as a soldier in the Revolutionary War, visit Washington Crossing Historic Park, in Bucks County, or Brandywine Battlefield in Chadds Ford, Delaware County.

An encampment at Brandywine Battlefield. PENNSYLVANIA HISTORICAL AND MUSEUM COMMISSION

1 egg, beaten

1 cup buttermilk

¹/₄ cup shortening

Mix ingredients in order. Do not overmix. Bake in a greased 9x13x2 pan in a 400-degree oven until done, about 20 minutes, depending on the size of the pan. This may also be cooked in a cast-iron skillet on a stovetop. Slice and serve with butter. Makes 6 servings.

Erie Maritime Museum and U.S. Brig Niagara

Whole Wheat Bread

$^1/_3$ cup plus I tablespoon brown sugar

2 cups warm water

I package dry yeast

5 to 6 cups whole wheat flour

$^3/_4$ cup powdered milk

2 teaspoons salt

$^1/_3$ cup vegetable oil

Dissolve 1 tablespoon brown sugar in water and add yeast. Let mixture stand. Put 4 cups flour, powdered milk, remaining brown sugar, and salt in large bowl. Mix well. Add yeast mixture and oil to flour. Mix and knead. Knead in rest of flour until dough is smooth and elastic. Place in greased bowl, turning to grease entire ball. Let rest for 30 minutes, then knead down and form into loaves. Put in greased loaf pans. Let rise until doubled in size. Bake in a 375-degree oven for 35 minutes. Remove from pans and brush shortening or oil over entire surface of each loaf. Makes 2 loaves.

Washington Crossing Historic Park

Pumpkin Bread

I cup corn oil

4 eggs, beaten

$^2/_3$ cup water

2 cups canned pumpkin

$3^1/_3$ cups sifted flour

$1^1/_2$ teaspoons salt

I teaspoon nutmeg

I teaspoon cinnamon

2 teaspoons baking soda

3 cups sugar

$^1/_2$ cup raisins

$^1/_2$ cup chopped nuts

Grease and flour two long loaf pans or three standard loaf pans. In a bowl, mix together flour, salt, nutmeg, cinnamon, baking soda, and sugar. In another bowl, mix oil, eggs, water, and pumpkin. Add dry ingredients to wet ones, then add raisins and nuts. Bake 1 hour at 350 degrees. Will stay moist for days. Makes 2 or 3 loaves.

Hope Lodge

Mush Muffins

2 cups cooked mush
1 cup warm milk
2 teaspoons sugar
2 teaspoons salt
1 tablespoon butter
5 to 6 cups flour
$^1/_2$ teaspoon dry yeast

Mix milk, sugar, salt, and butter with fresh cooked mush. Let cool to lukewarm. Mix yeast with flour, and add to the mush mixture to make a moderately stiff dough. Let rise overnight in a cool place. Next morning, punch down the dough and roll out on a board about an inch thick or a little less. Cut rounds with a biscuit cutter or drinking glass. Let rise on a floured board. Bake on a hot greased griddle until brown. Turn and bake on the other side. Makes 4 to 6 servings.

Homemade Mush

1 cup roasted cornmeal
$^1/_2$ cup warm water
2 cups cold water
1$^1/_2$ teaspoons salt

Mix cornmeal with the warm water to make a paste. Add salt to cold water and bring to boil. Remove from heat and add paste gradually. Cook over low heat for $^1/_2$ hour.

Daniel Boone Homestead

Rexmont Coffee Cake

1 cup sugar
2 cups flour
2$^1/_2$ teaspoons baking powder
1 cup milk (or more)
melted butter, shortening, or salad oil
1 egg (optional)
brown sugar
cinnamon

Mix together first five ingredients, along with an egg, if desired. Pour batter into two greased 9-inch glass pie dishes. Top with lots of brown sugar, then sprinkle with cinnamon. Bake in 350-degree oven for about 25 minutes.

Cornwall Iron Furnace

Main Dishes

Wiltshire Pork Pie

3 cups flour

pinch salt

3/4 cup unsalted butter

2–2 1/2 tablespoons ice water

1/2 ounce butter

I onion, chopped

2 rashers (6 pieces) of nicely marbled bacon, rind removed, then chopped

I pound belly of pork, chopped (or substitute ground pork)

I small cooking apple, peeled and chopped

2 to 3 ounces cheddar cheese, diced

2 tablespoons chopped fresh parsley

I teaspoon chopped fresh sage

salt and pepper to taste

pinch dry mustard

I egg, beaten

small sprig of sage (for garnish)

Mix salt into flour and cut in cold butter with fingers or pastry cutter. Add ice water until dough has formed single ball. Wrap in plastic and refrigerate for at least 30 minutes. Roll out the pastry on a lightly floured surface. Divide in half, and use half to line a lightly greased 9-inch pie plate. Melt butter in a frying pan, and lightly fry onion and bacon. Add pork and cook for 15 to 20 minutes, stirring frequently. Let cool, then stir in apple, cheese, herbs, and seasonings, adding sufficient beaten egg to bind the mixture. Preheat oven to 425 degrees. Fill pie shell with pork mixture, and top with remaining pastry, sealing edges well and trimming neatly. Make a steam hole, and decorate with pastry leaves. Brush with remaining beaten egg to glaze. Bake for 15 minutes, then reduce temperature to 350 degrees and bake an additional 25 to 30 minutes, until the pie is golden brown. Serve hot or cold, garnished with sage. Makes 4 to 6 servings.

Joseph Priestley House

Left: *Graeme Park.* KYLE R. WEAVER

35

Scrapple (Pannhaas)

2 pig hearts

1 1/2 pounds pig liver

2 pounds somewhat fatty pork

2 or 3 pounds pork bones (optional)

1/2 cup flour

1 cup buckwheat flour

3 cups yellow cornmeal

2 tablespoons salt

2 tablespoons ground black pepper

1 1/2 tablespoons ground sage (optional)

Cover bones and meat completely with water in a large pot. Boil for 3 hours. Remove meat and bones, and let cool. Strain the liquid and set aside. Cut off excess fat and gristle, then grind the meat. Discard bones. Mix together the flours and cornmeal. Dissolve a little of the flour mixture in some of the liquid to make a smooth paste. Mix this into the rest of the liquid, add meat, and bring to a boil. Take it off the heat, and stir in the rest of the flour-cornmeal mixture and seasonings. Adjust seasonings to taste. Return to the heat and boil for 30 to 45 minutes, or until very thick. The mixture must be stirred constantly after the cornmeal is added, as it will burn very easily. When a cake tester remains upright in the mixture, pour into bread pans and let cool. After refrigerating overnight, the scrapple will be ready to fry. If it is cooked nice and thick, it will slice easily and fry without falling apart. Fry on both sides in a skillet with a little lard or butter. You may dip the scrapple into flour before frying. In the Cambria–Somerset County area, scrapple is often topped with maple syrup, jelly, or apple butter. In Lancaster County, where Landis Valley Museum is located, the preferred topping is King Syrup, molasses, or ketchup. Makes 3 to 4 servings.

Landis Valley Museum

Lumber Camp Skillet

2 strips bacon

3 cups red potatoes, scrubbed and cut in 1/4-inch slices

1 cup sliced bell peppers

1 cup chopped onions

2 cups whole-kernel corn, fresh, frozen, or canned

1 pound precooked smoked andouille or other sausage, cut in 1/2-inch slices

salt and pepper

cayenne pepper

Fry bacon in large pan until crisp. Remove from pan, leaving bacon drippings. Add potatoes, peppers, and onions, and stir-fry over medium-low heat until potatoes start to soften. Add corn and sausage, and continue to stir-fry until potatoes are done and mixture is heated through. Add crumbled bacon. Season to taste. Makes 6 servings. *Note:* Olive oil may be substituted for bacon drippings.

Pennsylvania Lumber Museum

Cornish Pasties

2 recipes piecrust (see below)
8 ounces sirloin or other lean tender beef
2 medium potatoes, peeled and chopped fine
1/2 cup finely chopped onion
grated turnip, carrot, or chopped mushroom (optional)
salt and thyme to taste
3 tablespoons cold water

Roll out pastry to 1/4 inch thick. Cut into 4 rounds, using saucer or saucepan lid. Cut meat into small pieces. Mix meat, potato, and onion together, adding vegetables (if desired), seasonings, and water. Place a quarter of the meat mixture on one half of a circle of pastry. Dampen edges of pastry with cold water, and fold over to cover the mixture. Press the edges together, and twist to make a ropelike effect. Make 2 or 3 slits in the side. Brush with beaten egg or milk, and place on a sheet pan. Bake about 30 minutes at 350 degrees, then another 15 to 20 minutes at 300 degrees, until golden brown. Makes 4 pasties.

Piecrust

6 tablespoons unsalted butter, cold
1 cup plus 1 tablespoon pastry flour or bleached all-purpose flour
1/8 teaspoon salt
1/8 teaspoon baking powder
1/4 cup cream cheese, cold
1 tablespoon ice water
1 1/2 teaspoons cider vinegar

Cut the butter up into small chips. Chill in the freezer. Blend the dry ingredients together in large stainless bowl. Work cream cheese into the dry mix until the consistency of coarse meal. Cut in butter until the size of small peas. Add ice water and vinegar and blend until just incorporated (a food processor works well for this). Chill till ready to roll out. Keeps in refrigerator for 2 days, in the freezer for 3 months.

Museum of Anthracite Mining

THE PENNSYLVANIA DUTCH TRADITION

About 75,000 German-speaking immigrants accepted William Penn's invitation to come to Pennsylvania between 1683 and 1820. Leaving behind religious persecution and economic hardship, they found some of the richest farming soil in the New World in southeastern Pennsylvania. By 1790, the Pennsylvania "Dutch" made up about 40 percent of the state's population, many of them living in Berks and Lancaster Counties. The Landis Valley Museum in Lancaster County, the largest museum of Pennsylvania Dutch life in the country, showcases and interprets their culture, including their foodways.

The Pennsylvania Dutch have made significant contributions to food traditions in Pennsylvania and across America. Traditional Pennsylvania Dutch cooking features the interplay between sweet and salty flavors, such as in schnitz un knepp (page 59) and gumbis (page 41), and between sweets and sours. Many food dishes that remain popular to this day are associated with the Pennsylvania Dutch, including pretzels, sauerkraut, fasnachts, liverwurst, scrapple (page 36), and dandelion salad.

Fermented cabbage, known as sauerkraut (page 69), was enjoyed throughout the year and is still traditionally served with pork on New Year's Day to ensure good luck in the coming year. When the Confederate Army captured the town of Chambersburg in 1863, they demanded twenty-five barrels of sauerkraut from the town's residents. The town's leaders thought it was a trick until they realized the Rebel soldiers were suffering from scurvy, for which sauerkraut offered nutritional relief.

Fasnachts (a potato-based doughnut) are prepared on Shrove Tuesday, often referred to as Fasnacht Day. They represent a last-minute indulgence before the austerity of the Lenten season, as well as a way of using up the lard in the house.

Pennsylvania Dutch cooking, with its roots in Pennsylvania's past, has become a significant part of modern cuisine.

Landis family reunion at the Pennsylvania Farm Museum, c. 1940. LANDIS VALLEY MUSEUM

Pig Stomach

1 pig stomach, cleaned and rinsed

2 pounds skinless sausage

5 pounds potatoes, cubed

1 or 2 small onions, diced

salt and pepper to taste

Sew one end of opening in pig stomach shut with needle and thread. Mix sausage, potatoes, onions, and seasonings. Stuff mixture into stomach. Sew other end of stomach shut. Place in roasting pan with 1 inch of water in bottom. Bake at 350 degrees for 3 hours. Pig stomach often was served as a Christmas or holiday dinner. Frequently it was the first fresh meat of the winter season. Using the stomach shows the frugality of the Pennsylvania Dutch, who often said, "Everything from the pig can be used except the squeal." Makes 6 to 8 servings.

Landis Valley Museum

Bouquet's Bounty

2 pounds beef

2 tablespoons butter

3 cups hot water

1 clove garlic

2 tablespoons vinegar

1 teaspoon molasses

1 large onion, sliced

2 bay leaves

1 tablespoon salt

1 teaspoon sugar

1/2 teaspoon pepper

1/2 teaspoon paprika

6 carrots, pared and cut

4 potatoes, peeled and quartered

2 cups peas

4 tablespoons flour

1/2 cup water

Cut meat into cubes and brown in butter. Add water, garlic, vinegar, molasses, onion, and seasonings. Simmer 1 1/2 hours. Remove bay leaves and garlic. Add carrots and potatoes. Cook 45 minutes. Add peas and cook a few more minutes. Mix flour and water, and stir into bounty. Makes 4 to 6 servings. *Note:* This is an original recipe from the 60th Royal American Regiment of Foot, French and Indian War reenactors.

Fort Pitt Museum and Bushy Run Battlefield

Bedford Stew

**2 whole chicken breasts (you'll need 2 cups for this recipe;
there will be some left over)**

celery, onion, seasonings to taste

2 quarts water

¹/4 cup chopped onion

3 tablespoons butter or margarine

3 tablespoons flour

¹/2 teaspoon salt

I cup peas

3-ounce can sliced mushrooms, drained

I cup corn

I ¹/2 cups cooked potatoes, diced

Cook chicken breasts in water with celery, onions, and seasonings. Remove chicken when done, reserving 1¹/2 cups of the broth. Debone and coarsely chop the meat, and set aside. Cook chopped onion in butter until tender. Blend in flour and salt. Add reserved broth all at once; cook and stir until thickened and bubbly. Add chicken and vegetables; heat until bubbling. Makes 6 servings. *Note:* Instead of making the broth from scratch, you can use 1¹/2 cups canned chicken broth and 2 cups cooked chicken, coarsely chopped. Recipe from 60th Royal American Regiment of Foot reenactors.

Fort Pitt Museum

Sausage

12 pounds meat (pork or beef)

3 tablespoons salt

3 tablespoons black pepper

5 to 8 tablespoons sage

12 feet of casings

Mix all ingredients together well, and put into casings. *Note:* The original recipe came from John Baer's 1864 *Almanac,* Lancaster, Pennsylvania. You may prefer coriander as a seasoning. Use 3 to 4 tablespoons. You can fry a bit and taste to see if the seasonings suit your taste. Do not eat uncooked sausage.

Landis Valley Museum

Gumbis

1 large head cabbage
butter
3 or 4 small onions
3 or 4 medium apples
water or ham broth
$^1/_4$ to $^1/_2$ pound chopped, cooked ham or bacon (optional)

Remove one or two of the large outer leaves from cabbage to serve as a lid for
your stewpot. Cut up the rest of the cabbage in bite-size pieces. Fry in a little
butter to wilt it down, then set aside. Slice onions into rings, and set aside. Peel
apples and slice into quarters or eighths; set aside. In a large ovenproof stewpot
or Dutch oven, layer the foods, starting with cabbage, then a layer of onions,
then another layer of cabbage, and then a layer of apples. Ham or bacon can
also be added as the dish is assembled. Continue to layer the cabbage, onions,
and apples, ending with the reserved cabbage leaves. Fill pot with water or ham
broth. Bake in 350-degree oven for 1 hour. Other meats, such as venison or rabbit, can be used, as can other fruits, such as fresh or dried pears or peaches.
Makes 4 to 6 servings. *Note:* If you are cooking on an open hearth, place the
stewpot on a brick or trivet in the fireplace and surround with hot coals. Let
cook for several hours.

Daniel Boone Homestead

Venison Pie

1 1/2 pounds leg or shoulder of venison
2 ounces salt pork, blanched and drained
1/2 pound mushrooms, trimmed and sliced
2 tablespoons butter
1 1/2 tablespoons flour
salt and freshly ground pepper

Marinade

1 onion
1 celery rib
7 coriander seeds
7 whole allspice or juniper berries
2 bay leaves
2 sprigs parsley
pinch marjoram
1 cup red wine
5 tablespoons olive oil

Pastry

2 cups flour
1/2 teaspoon salt
1/4 pound butter
3 tablespoons lard
2 egg yolks
2 tablespoons cold water
1 egg, lightly beaten

Cut venison into 1-inch cubes, removing all gristle. Prepare the vegetables and spices for the marinade: peel and finely chop the onion, wash the celery and chop it finely, and crush the coriander seeds and allspice or juniper berries. Layer venison in large bowl with vegetables and seasonings, and pour in wine mixed with oil. Cover bowl with plastic wrap and allow meat to marinate in refrigerator for at least 8 hours.

Precook pie filling to avoid overbaking the pastry. Dice salt pork, and sauté over low heat to extract all the fat. Add butter to pan, together with mushrooms. Blend in enough flour to absorb all the fat, and cook this roux for about 3 minutes.

When meat is done marinating, remove and strain through a sieve, reserving liquid. Gradually blend marinade liquid into roux, add venison, and bring sauce to a boil. Thin with a little water, if necessary, and season to taste with salt and pepper. Cover pan with tight-fitting lid, and simmer over low heat for 1 1/2 hours. Adjust seasonings. Leave meat to cool while making pastry.

Sift flour and salt into a mixing bowl. Cut in butter and lard until mixture has consistency of bread crumbs. Beat egg yolks with water, and blend into flour. Knead dough until it leaves the sides of the bowl clean, adding more water if necessary. Cover the kneaded dough with waxed paper, and refrigerate for at least 1 hour.

Spoon cooled meat and sauce into a deep pie dish or baking dish, setting a pastry funnel or inverted egg cup in the center. Roll out pastry on a floured surface to a thickness of 1/4 inch. Cut off 1/2-inch-wide strips, and place them on the moistened rim of the pie dish. Brush with water before covering filling with remaining pastry. Seal pastry edges, and trim with a knife. Scallop the edges, and brush pastry with lightly beaten egg; decorate with leaves cut from pastry trimmings, and brush leaves with more egg. Make a few small slits in top of pastry for steam to escape.

Bake in center of preheated oven at 425 degrees for 20 minutes, then reduce heat to 375 degrees and bake for 30 minutes more, or until pie is golden brown. Makes 6 servings.

Daniel Boone Homestead

Roast Beef

4- to 5-pound beef brisket (or similar cut of meat)

salt and pepper to taste

1 bottle burgundy red wine

1 medium onion

1 tablespoon fresh chopped parsley

1/2 tablespoon fresh grated ginger

bouquet of fine herbs, dried or fresh: tarragon, chervil, marjoram, rosemary, thyme

1 pound carrots, chopped

1 pound seedless grapes, any variety

2 tablespoons sugar

Season meat with salt and pepper, and place in a pot. Cover meat with wine. Add onion, parsley, ginger, and fine herbs. Let simmer for 2 to 4 hours, depending on the size of the meat. Add carrots 1 1/2 hours before meat is done simmering. To prepare glaze for meat, crush grapes and strain through a cloth. Pour juice and sugar into a pan, and dissolve the sugar. Heat until juice thickens. When meat has finished cooking, lay on a serving platter, and arrange carrots around it. Pour glaze over meat and serve. Makes 6 to 8 servings.

Old Economy Village

HUNTING WITH DANIEL BOONE

Although Daniel Boone (1734–1820) is often associated with North Carolina, Kentucky, West Virginia, and Missouri, he was born and raised in the Oley Valley of Pennsylvania near Reading, Berks County.

At the time the Boone family arrived in the Oley Valley, the land was still a frontier, and the area was a melting pot of various European immigrants and Indian tribes. During his adolescence, Daniel gained valuable outdoor skills, including hunting and trapping, in the dense Pennsylvania forest. This experience would be pivotal to his legendary exploits later in life. Until a pioneer family could establish a farm, it depended on hunting, fishing, and trapping for survival. Turkeys, deer, rabbits, pheasants, ruffed grouse, partridge, and other small game served as food for the dinner table.

The kitchen at the Daniel Boone Homestead.

CRAIG A. BENNER

When Daniel turned twelve, he received his first firearm, a short-barreled rifle. Hunting was permitted on all the commonwealth's lands from 1683 by William Penn. The first formal hunting regulations were put into effect in 1721 by provincial governor Sir William Keith, who instituted a deer season from January 1 to July 1 (Native Americans were exempt), allowed improved lands to be put off bounds to hunters by their owners, and outlawed the hunting of "pigeon, dove, partridge or other fowl" in the city of Philadelphia.

Around 1750, the Boone family moved to North Carolina, and William Maugridge, a cousin of Daniel's father and a friend of Benjamin Franklin, purchased the Boone homestead. A November 3 letter from Benjamin Franklin's wife, Deborah, to her husband commented, "Speaking of buckwheat cakes, our good friend Mr. Maugridge has sent some of the best flour that I ever saw and we had them hot" (see raised buckwheat griddle cakes, page 30).

From about 1770 to 1831, John DeTurk and his son Abraham worked the soil and raised their families at the homestead. DeTurk family inventories reveal the animals and plants raised on the farm, as well as items that were used to hunt or trap and to process the food. The inventories include wheat, corn, buckwheat, rye, and oats. Other items listed were a teapot, cabbage tub, grindstone, half barrel of mackerels, and fishing rod.

In 1779, the DeTurks replaced the walls of the original one-story log home with a larger two-story stone structure but left the original foundation and spring cellar intact. They can still be viewed today.

Today the Daniel Boone Homestead, Birdsboro, Berks County, showcases the families that called the farm home. Cooking demonstrations showcase the foodways of the three families who lived here during the eighteenth century, including dishes of goose, squirrel, venison (page 42), and even groundhog.

Dried Lima Beans and Sausage

I pound dried lima beans
$1/2$ pound fresh pork sausage, cooked
salt and pepper to taste

Wash and soak lima beans overnight. Do not drain. Cook beans until almost done. Crumble in cooked sausage and continue to cook until creamy. Season with salt and pepper. More sausage can be added and served as a main dish over sippets, small pieces of toast or bread soaked in gravy. Makes 4 servings.

Graeme Park

Dried Corn and Fresh Sausage Stew

I cup dried corn
2 cups boiling water
I pound fresh sausage, cooked
4 medium potatoes, diced
milk
salt and pepper to taste

Soak dried corn overnight in boiling water, then cook seasoned with salt for about 1 hour, adding water as needed. Cut cooked sausage into $1/2$-inch pieces, and add to corn together with diced potatoes and milk to cover. Cook over medium heat until potatoes are soft, about 20 to 25 minutes, adding more milk if desired. Season with salt and pepper to taste. Makes 4 to 6 servings. *Note:* Instead of dried corn, you can use leftover corn from a previous meal.

Graeme Park

Sausage and Apples

I pound pork sausage links
$1/4$ cup cider
6 medium cooking apples, sliced
brown sugar (optional)

This simple dish is very satisfying. In a large pan, begin frying cut pieces of sausage. When well browned, add cider and continue to cook. When meat is just about cooked through, add apple slices and cook until apples are softened. For those who like foods on the sweet side, a little brown sugar can be added. Makes 4 to 6 servings.

Daniel Boone Homestead

Young Chicken Fricassee

2 chicken breast halves
2 tablespoons butter
salt
small bunch parsley
small bunch basil
1 teaspoon thyme
1 or 2 lemons
1 onion

Preheat oven to 350 degrees. Lay cleaned chicken in baking pan. Slice butter and lay pats throughout pan. Season chicken with salt. Lay parsley, basil, and thyme on chicken. Slice lemons and place on meat. Cut onion in large pieces and lay throughout pan. Add 1/8 inch water to pan. Cover and cook for 30 minutes. Then remove herbs and squeeze out both. Remove chicken and place on a platter. Reserve leftover broth and drippings in pan for sauce. Makes 2 servings.

Sauce

reserved chicken broth
2 eggs
1/2 cup dry white wine or sherry
1 heaping tablespoon flour
1/4 teaspoon grated nutmeg

Continue cooking reserved chicken broth in pan on burner. In mixing bowl, whisk eggs and wine together. Slowly add some broth to eggs, to temper them. When eggs and wine are warmed, add mixture back into pan on burner. Whisk the mixture, and add flour and nutmeg. Keep heating and stirring until the sauce thickens. Pour over chicken.

Old Economy Village

Halupki (Polish)

1 head of cabbage

Filling

1 cup uncooked rice
2 cups water
2 pounds ground beef
1 onion, chopped

¹/₄ cup fresh parsley, chopped

salt

pepper

2 eggs

Sauce

1 tablespoon vinegar

1 can tomato puree

cabbage water

Cook cabbage leaves and drain. Set liquid aside. Cook rice in water for 5 minutes. Combine ground beef, onion, parsley, salt, and pepper. Add rice to meat mixture. Add eggs. Place small amount of mixture on cabbage leaf and roll up. Place in small roaster pan. Mix vinegar into tomato puree and pour over cabbage rolls. Add just enough cabbage water to cover. Cook for 1 hour at 325 degrees. Makes 6 servings.

Anthracite Heritage Museum
Eckley Miners' Village

U.S. Brig *Niagara* Lunch Casserole

¹/₂ cup margarine

¹/₂ cup flour

2 cups chicken bouillon

2 cups milk

¹/₄ cup hot sauce

seasoned salt and pepper to taste

6¹/₄ cups cooked rice

3 cups chicken, cooked and diced

8 ounces canned mushrooms with liquid, chopped

4 ounces pimiento, chopped

¹/₄ cup parsley, chopped

1 small onion, chopped

³/₄ cup stale bread cubes, buttered

Melt margarine and blend in flour. Stir in bouillon and milk, and cook, stirring until thickened. Add hot sauce, seasoned salt, and pepper to taste. Mix with rice and all remaining ingredients except bread cubes. Pour into baking pan and top with bread cubes. Bake at 375 degrees for 10 minutes, or until piping hot. Makes 12 to 13 servings. *Note:* A hearty casserole served to the modern-day crew of the *Niagara* and prepared in the oven of the woodstove on board.

Erie Maritime Museum and U.S. Brig Niagara

THE ETHNIC MIXING BOWL

Pennsylvania's cultural diversity is reflected in its rich culinary heritage. Many ethnic groups are represented, including Native Americans; the early Swedish, English, and German settlers; the rich infusion of Eastern and Southern European settlers; Latinos; and African Americans. Pennsylvania's diversification continues to the present with a myriad of new immigrants from all over the world. From the earliest days of the colony to the present, immigrants have enriched the commonwealth with foodways from their native lands.

Early settlers from the British Isles brought their traditions and, where they had access to nearby ports, often imported foodstuffs from overseas. The recipes served at Graeme Park, home of Colonial governor William Keith in Horsham, Montgomery County, reflect this British heritage and the home's access to the port of Philadelphia and its trade goods. Scones (page 19), Scotch eggs (page 7), and colcannon (page 78) reflect these influences. The British influence extended to Cornwall Iron Furnace, in Lebanon County, where the ironworkers enjoyed mince meat pies (page 91). While the hard labor of Pennsylvania's coal miners helped build a nation, the immigration of workers from Ireland, England, Wales, Hungary, Austria, Poland, Lithuania, Italy, Russia, Germany, and many other countries also brought a rich diversity to Pennsylvania's table, including pierogies (page 26), holiday ricotta cheese bread (page 28), and halupki (page 46).

At the end of a day in the mines, workers returned home to the wonderful smells of corned beef and cabbage, sausage, sauerkraut, pasties, and pasta. The kitchen was the center of family life where children played and laundry, sewing, and even

Workers with lunch pails descend into a mine. ANTHRACITE HERITAGE MUSEUM

bathing took place. Family talks, school homework for children not yet working in the mines, and discussions of politics and miners' rights all took place at the kitchen table with the warmth of the coal stove nearby.

Although the mine owners hoped to weaken the influence of labor unions by bringing in workers who did not speak English when they arrived, they also inadvertently enriched the culture of the coal region. Immigrants became part of the rich culture of the area, and their ethnic traditions—including their foods—became part of the wide-ranging ethnic mix that created Pennsylvania's diversity.

The Anthracite Heritage Museum in Scranton, Lackawanna County, is open year-round for visitors to learn about the lives of miners and see re-creations of family homes, kitchens, pubs, and churches. Eckley Miners' Village in Carbon County is a real-life company town, and the Museum of Anthracite Mining in Schuylkill County adds to our understanding of the life of miners.

A kitchen at Eckley Miners' Village. CRAIG A. BENNER

Kedgere

4 tablespoons butter
¹/₂ small zucchini, sliced
2 onions, sliced
I small green pepper, sliced
¹/₂ cup pineapple chunks
I small mango
2 teaspoons flour
2 teaspoons curry powder
I teaspoon tomato paste
2 cups shredded coconut
2¹/₂ cups chicken broth
I pound cooked salmon or haddock
I¹/₂ cups cooked rice
4 hard-boiled eggs

Melt butter, add vegetables and fruits, and cook for 10 minutes. Sprinkle flour over mixture to thicken. Stir in curry powder, tomato paste, and coconut. Add chicken broth, and simmer 30 minutes. Add fish, rice, and eggs. Makes 4 servings.

Museum of Anthracite Mining

Irish Corned Beef and Cabbage

4- to 5-pound corned beef brisket
$^1/_2$ teaspoon Tabasco sauce
1 onion, sliced
1 bay leaf
$^1/_2$ teaspoon dried rosemary
1 celery rib
1 pared carrot
1 sprig parsley
1 head green cabbage

Place brisket in large deep kettle; cover with cold water. Add Tabasco sauce, onion, bay leaf, rosemary, celery, carrot, and parsley. Cover and bring to a boil. Then reduce heat and simmer for 4 to 5 hours. Wash cabbage and cut into quarters. A half hour before beef is done, skim excess fat from top of liquid and place cabbage on beef. Cover and simmer for 15 minutes, or until cabbage is just crisp tender. Makes 6 servings.

Eckley Miners' Village

Stuffed Cabbage (Sarma)

whole cabbage
salt
vinegar

Make a few incisions at the top of the cabbage, put it on a large fork, and dip into boiling water into which some salt and vinegar have been added. Turn cabbage over and over until leaves fall off, then leave in boiling water for a few more seconds. Take cabbage out, cut hard part off, and place leaves on board ready for filling.

Filling

2 onions
lard or bacon grease
$^1/_2$ pound each ground beef and pork
1 egg
1 clove garlic, crushed
salt and pepper
paprika
$^1/_2$ cup rice, parboiled 3 to 4 minutes

Chop onions and brown in lard or bacon grease. Mix together ground meats thoroughly. Add egg, onions, garlic, salt, pepper, paprika, and rice. Place a nice-size portion on each leaf. Roll up leaves after stuffing, and secure each with a toothpick. Shred the smaller leaves and put some on the bottom of a baking dish, then put in the cabbage rolls, and add some more shredded cabbage on top of the rolls.

Sauce and Gravy

1 tablespoon tomato paste

³/₄ cup beef stock or bouillon

several strips of bacon

1 tablespoon shortening

1 tablespoon flour

1 cup water

1 teaspoon sweet paprika

sour cream

parsley (optional)

Combine the tomato paste with the beef stock or bouillon, and pour over cabbage rolls to cover. Place a few uncooked bacon strips on top. Bake for 45 minutes to 1 hour in a 375-degree oven, or cook in a crockpot on low for 7 to 9 hours. When almost done, add some brown gravy made from flour browned in shortening to which you've added water and paprika. Place cabbage rolls on platter, and top each with a dollop of sour cream and parsley. Makes 4 to 6 servings. *Note:* A Slovak family recipe from Ann Karincs of Cornwall.

Cornwall Iron Furnace

Baked Shad

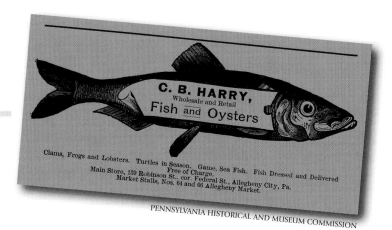

PENNSYLVANIA HISTORICAL AND MUSEUM COMMISSION

4 fillets of fresh boned shad

1 cup water

¹/₄ cup white wine

¹/₂ cup clarified butter

paprika

juice of ¹/₂ lemon

parsley (for garnish)

Place shad fillets on buttered baking dish. Mix together water, wine, and clarified butter, and pour over fish. Sprinkle with paprika. Bake at 325 degrees for 12 to 15 minutes. Finish with lemon juice. Serve with fresh chopped parsley. Makes 4 servings.

Washington Crossing Historic Park

Chicken Pot Pie

3- to 4-pound whole chicken
2 quarts water
1 teaspoon salt
pinch saffron
3 to 4 potatoes, diced
3 carrots, coarsely cubed
2 small onions, diced

Cook chicken in salted water with saffron until tender. Remove chicken to cool. To the boiling broth, add potatoes, carrots, and onion. Cook for 15 minutes. Debone cooled chicken and set aside.

Pot Pie Dough

1 1/4 cups flour
1/2 teaspoon salt
1 teaspoon baking powder
1 egg
3 tablespoons water

Combine flour, salt, and baking powder. Beat eggs with water. With a fork, work into flour and salt to make a stiff dough. Add more water if mix is too dry. Roll dough out onto a floured board until thin, and cut into 2-inch squares. Drop dough squares into boiling broth a few at a time, and cook about 20 more minutes. Stir in chicken pieces and heat through. Makes 6 servings.

Landis Valley Museum

Shad and Shad Roe in Cream

2 boned shad fillets, about 2 pounds
2 pairs shad roe
salt and freshly ground pepper
4 tablespoons butter
2 tablespoons finely chopped shallots
1 cup heavy cream, divided
juice of 1/2 lemon
2 tablespoons finely chopped parsley or chives

Cut fillets in half lengthwise. Season fillets and roe with salt and pepper. Heat butter in large heavy skillet, and add shad and roe in one layer. Sprinkle shallots between pieces of shad and roe. Add 1/2 cup heavy cream to skillet and cover. Bring to a boil and cook for 10 to 15 minutes. Uncover and remove the

Shad fishing on the Delaware River in the nineteenth century. PENNSYLVANIA STATE ARCHIVES

fish to a serving platter. Split the roe in half, and top each portion of fish with a piece of roe. Add the remaining 1/2 cup heavy cream to the skillet and bring to a boil. Put sauce through a fine sieve into a saucepan. Bring to a boil and simmer 5 minutes. Add lemon juice and more salt and pepper to taste. Pour the sauce over the fish and roe. Sprinkle with parsley or chives. Makes 4 servings.

Washington Crossing Historic Park

Shad Roe with Bacon

1 pair shad roe
bacon

Fry several strips of bacon in a skillet until golden brown. Remove bacon and cook shad roe in bacon fat for 3 to 4 minutes per side. Cover and cook another 5 minutes on low heat. Serve with bacon if desired. Makes 2 servings.

Washington Crossing Historic Park

AMERICAN SHAD: AN IMPORTANT FISH

Pennsylvania's abundance of rivers, streams, and lakes offered an important resource to the colonists of Penn's Woods. Native Americans taught them about the native fish and how to catch them—trout, paddlefish, eel, bass, and especially American shad. Shad were harvested during the annual spring spawning runs, generally occurring between February and June, and the colonists learned how to catch and preserve them. Flavorful and nutritious, any fish not eaten (see shad recipes on pages 51 and 52) could be salted and preserved for the winter months. Abundant in the Delaware and Susquehanna Rivers, shad also provided employment for various supporting industries, such as net, boat, and wagon makers; carpenters; and fish sellers. Shad even served as a form of currency traded for oil, salt, whiskey, and labor.

During the Revolutionary War, shad was abundant on the Delaware River and its tributaries, and dried shad might have been included in the three days' rations George Washington and his troops took when they crossed the Delaware on December 25, 1776, in preparation for the attack on the British at Trenton. In the spring of 1778, following their bitter winter encampment at Valley Forge, Washington and his troops feasted on shad caught from the Schuylkill River, the largest tributary to the Delaware. The early spring run of American shad that year has been credited with helping save the Continental Army from starvation.

Washington Crossing Historic Park on the Delaware River in Bucks County interprets Washington's crossing and the historic village of Taylorsville.

Hungarian Veal Goulash

2 tablespoons lard

1 large onion, sliced

2 pounds veal shoulder, cut into 1- to 2-inch cubes

2 tablespoons flour

2 cups hot soup stock or water

1/8 teaspoon marjoram

3 teaspoons paprika

salt and pepper

4 potatoes, diced

Heat lard and brown onion in it. Dredge veal in flour, and brown in hot lard. Add seasonings and stock or water. Cover and cook for 1/2 hour. Add potatoes, and cook until both veal and potatoes are done, about 1/2 hour longer. To serve, thicken liquid with flour blended into cold water. Makes 4 to 6 servings.

Cornwall Iron Furnace

Hungarian Goulash with Potatoes

3 tablespoons fat or salad oil

3 cups thinly sliced onions

6 teaspoons paprika, divided

1 1/2 pounds beef round or chuck, cut in 1-inch cubes

3 cups water

2 1/4 teaspoons salt

4 pared medium potatoes, quartered

The night before, heat fat or oil in deep, covered skillet or Dutch oven. Add onions and salt, and cook, tossing occasionally with a fork, until onions are a deep golden brown. Stir in 1 1/2 teaspoons paprika, then add beef. Cover tightly and simmer 1 hour. Add remaining 4 1/2 teaspoons paprika and water; cover and cook 1/2 hour longer. Cool, then store, covered, in refrigerator until dinnertime the next day. To serve, heat goulash to the boiling point; add quartered potatoes and cook, covered, about 1/2 hour, or until meat and potatoes are tender. *Note:* If preferred, omit potatoes and serve with buttered noodles. Makes 5 servings.

Cornwall Iron Furnace

Hungarian Dumplings

1 cup sifted flour

1 1/2 teaspoons baking powder

1/2 teaspoon salt

1 egg, well beaten

1/2 cup milk

1 teaspoon melted butter

Sift together dry ingredients. Combine egg, milk, and butter. Add gradually to flour, stirring until dough is smooth and no longer sticks to spoon. Break off pieces of dough about 1 inch long and 1/2 inch thick, and drop into rapidly boiling water or soup. Boil, covered, for 12 to 15 minutes. Makes 12 small dumplings.

Cornwall Iron Furnace

Chicken Paprikash

8 strips of bacon
1/4 cup finely chopped onion
2 tablespoons fresh parsley
2 carrots, sliced
2 celery ribs, chopped
3/4 cup flour
1 1/2 teaspoons salt
1 1/2 teaspoons paprika
2 pounds boneless chicken breast, cut into 2x3-inch pieces
2 cups chicken stock

In large pan, sauté bacon, onion, parsley, carrots, and celery. Remove bacon strips. Place flour, salt, and paprika in a gallon-size bag. Shake to mix ingredients. Place chicken in bag and shake to coat. Brown chicken in hot pan. Reduce heat and add chicken stock. Simmer about 30 minutes, or until chicken is tender.

Sauce

4 tablespoons butter
4 tablespoons flour
2 cups chicken stock
1 1/2 cups milk
3 tablespoons paprika
3 cups sour cream

Cast ironware from Cornwall Iron Furnace.
CRAIG A. BENNER

In saucepan, melt butter and blend in flour. Heat until mixture bubbles, stirring constantly. Remove from heat, then add stock, milk, and paprika. Heat thoroughly over low heat. Stirring vigorously, gradually add sour cream to the sauce. Pour over chicken in skillet. Heat for 3 to 5 minutes, then turn off heat and leave for 1 hour, reheating before serving. Serve with spaetzel. Makes 4 to 5 servings.

Cornwall Iron Furnace

Chicken Fricassee

1 cut-up chicken

¹/₄ cup flour

3 teaspoons salt, divided

dash pepper

¹/₄ cup lard

4 cups boiling water or stock

1 large onion, chopped

few celery tops

2 carrots, finely chopped

few sprigs parsley

1 tomato or 1 tablespoon tomato paste

Add 2 teaspoons salt and pepper to flour and dredge chicken, turning each piece over and over until well coated. Heat lard in skillet or Dutch oven, and arrange floured chicken in it. Brown well on both sides, turning occasionally. Add water, onion, celery tops, carrots, parsley, tomato, and 1 teaspoon salt. Simmer, covered, about 1 hour, until a fork can be easily inserted in leg. Add more water if necessary. Remove chicken to heated platter, and keep warm while making gravy.

Gravy

1¹/₂ tablespoons flour

1 cup water or chicken stock

2 tablespoons cream

salt and pepper to taste

lemon juice or pinch dried tarragon

Mix flour into the stock left in the skillet for each cup of water or chicken stock and brown. Add the stock or boiling water and stir. Gradually add cream and keep stirring until thickened. Season with salt, pepper, and a little lemon juice or a pinch of dried tarragon. Place chicken in this gravy and serve warm. Makes 4 to 5 servings.

Cornwall Iron Furnace

Pennsylvania Dutch Potato Filling

6 large potatoes
1 large onion, chopped
1/2 cup diced celery, some leaves included
4 tablespoons butter or margarine
3 slices bread, toasted and cubed
1 cup milk
2 eggs
1 teaspoon salt
freshly ground pepper
3 tablespoons fresh chopped parsley

Peel and cut up potatoes; boil until tender. While potatoes are cooking, sauté onions and celery in butter, then add toast cubes and sauté until crisp. Drain and mash potatoes, adding milk as needed to mash. Beat in eggs, one at a time, beating well after each addition. Fold in sautéed vegetables and toast. Add salt, pepper, and parsley. Transfer into greased pan. Dot top with additional butter or margarine. Bake immediately at 350 degrees for about 1 hour, or at whatever temperature other foods in the oven require until puffed and brown. Makes 6 servings. *Note:* You may also add saffron, poultry seasoning, or even garlic.

Cornwall Iron Furnace

Nana's Filling

2 cups celery, chopped
2 cups onion, chopped
5 pounds potatoes, mashed
2 beaten eggs
1 to 2 cups milk
2 to 3 tablespoons shortening
10 to 12 ounces cubed bread

Add milk gradually to potatoes, and beat so mixture doesn't become too runny. Fry cubes of bread in shortening. Combine all ingredients and mix. Put in 9x13x2-inch pan. Dot with butter. Bake at 350 degrees for 1 hour, or until golden brown and "set." Makes 6 to 8 servings. *Note:* This filling was traditionally served at Thanksgiving, Christmas, and Easter.

Cornwall Iron Furnace

Schnitz un Knepp

3 pounds smoked ham
I quart tart dried apples (schnitz)
dumpling batter (below)

Boil ham in large kettle for about 2 hours, making sure there is always enough water to cover half. Soak schnitz in bowl, covered with water, for 2 hours. Add schnitz and water to ham kettle, and boil together for another hour. Drop in dumpling batter by tablespoonfuls. Continue to boil, covered, for 18 minutes without lifting lid.

Dumpling Batter

2 cups flour
4 teaspoons baking powder
$^1/_2$ teaspoon salt
I tablespoon shortening
I cup milk

Sift dry ingredients into bowl. Cut in shortening. Add milk slowly, mixing with a fork until well blended. Batter should be lumpy. Makes 6 servings.

Cornwall Iron Furnace

Young Chickens with Green Peas

4 or 5 chicken breasts
salt
2 tablespoons melted butter
several sprigs parsley, chopped
I package frozen green peas
I heaping tablespoon flour
1$^1/_2$ cups beef broth
a little sugar

Preheat oven to 350 degrees. Sprinkle chicken breasts with salt. Put butter and parsley in a 9x13-inch pan, and place chicken on top. Cover and roast at 350 degrees for 45 minutes. Add peas to meat and let roast for an additional 30 minutes. Lightly dust chicken with flour, and add beef broth. Sprinkle top with sugar, and bake an additional 15 minutes, or until golden brown. Serve with dumplings or spaetzel. Makes 4 to 5 servings. *Note:* Cooking time varies, depending on size of chicken; average is 1$^1/_2$ hours.

Old Economy Village

Large community feasts were prepared in the kitchen at Old Economy Village. ART BECKER

Good Meat Sausage

$^1/_4$-inch hog casings (about 3 yards)

$^1/_4$ teaspoon vinegar

1 cup water

3 pounds pork butt

2 teaspoons coarse salt

$^3/_4$ teaspoon finely ground white or black pepper

$^1/_2$ teaspoon dried thyme

$^1/_2$ teaspoon dried sage

$^1/_4$ teaspoon dried summer savory

$^3/_4$ teaspoon sugar

$^1/_2$ teaspoon crushed red pepper

Thoroughly wash hog casings inside and out. Soak in vinegar and water. Hog casings may remain in solution overnight or until ready to use. The vinegar solution softens the casings and makes them more transparent. Rinse well before stuffing. Cut pork butt into 1-inch cubes, then grind cubes. Mix all the seasonings in thoroughly with hands. Regrind meat. Stuff casings with meat mixture. Fry sausage in skillet until done. Uncooked or cooked sausage may be frozen, but keep links from touching each other. Makes 3 pounds.

Old Economy Village

Chicken Liver Sauté

$^1/_2$ pound chicken livers

butter

1 tablespoon flour

salt to taste

2 teaspoons thick meat sauce or gravy

1 tablespoon red wine

Clean livers and cut each in half. Sauté in butter in skillet over low heat until light brown, about 5 minutes, turning often. Remove livers; stir in flour. Stir in water gradually and heat until thickened, while stirring. Add salt, meat sauce or gravy, wine, and livers, and simmer for a few minutes. Serve over boiled noodles or toast. Makes 2 servings.

Cornwall Iron Furnace

Shreed Pyes (Lamb Pies)

2 cups cooked lamb, shredded in small pieces

3 dates, sliced

I apple, finely chopped

1/2 cup currants

I teaspoon caraway seed

I teaspoon cinnamon

1/4 teaspoon salt

2 tablespoons rose flower water

1/2 cup water or lamb broth

I piecrust

I egg yolk

I tablespoon water

Mix all but the last three ingredients in large bowl. Put mixture in 1 1/2-quart casserole, and cover with piecrust. Mix egg yolk with water, and brush on the crust. Bake at 350 degrees for 45 minutes. Makes 4 servings.

Pennsbury Manor

Sophie's Crispy Chicken

I chicken, cut up into parts (skinned or unskinned)

garlic salt

1/2 cup flour mixed with paprika to taste

2 eggs, beaten with a little milk

bread crumbs as needed

sunflower oil

Wash chicken and pat dry. Sprinkle with salt, and refrigerate at least 2 hours. Sprinkle with a little garlic salt. Dip in egg, dredge in flour-paprika mixture, and roll in bread crumbs. Lightly brown in sunflower oil. Place in jelly roll pan, and bake for 1 hour and 10 minutes at 375 degrees. Cover the last 1/2 hour if browning too quickly. Makes 4 to 6 servings.

Cornwall Iron Furnace

Chicken with Rice and Apricot Stuffing

5-pound whole chicken (or duck)
I small onion, chopped
I sprig parsley, chopped
I cup chopped celery
3 tablespoons oil or butter
3 cups fluffy boiled rice
$1/2$ teaspoon poultry seasoning
$1/4$ pound dried apricots
salt
5 tablespoons butter
flour (optional)

Rinse chicken or duck and remove any giblets. Place bird in roasting pan. Cook onion, parsley, and celery in oil in a skillet over medium-high heat for a few minutes. Add rice and poultry seasoning. Wash and dry apricots, then cut into strips with scissors and mix with rice. Stuff and truss bird, rub all over with butter, sprinkle with salt, and if desired, dust lightly with flour. Roast in 325-degree oven for $1^1/2$ hours. Serves 6 to 8. *Note:* Recipe from the Penn Fruit Company grocery store located in the Shop-a-rama shopping center, Levittown, Pennsylvania.

The State Museum of Pennsylvania

Spinaige (Spinach) Tart

9-inch piecrust
I package frozen chopped spinach
4 egg yolks
I cup cream
$1/4$ teaspoon salt
I teaspoon sugar
2 tablespoons melted butter

Prepare piecrust and bake in 400-degree oven for 5 minutes. Defrost and drain spinach. Beat egg yolks, then mix in rest of ingredients. Add drained spinach to this mixture and pour carefully into baked piecrust. Bake at 350 degrees for 35 to 40 minutes. Makes 6 servings.

Pennsbury Manor

WILLIAM PENN'S KITCHEN AND TABLE

Pennsbury Manor, Tullytown, Bucks County, the home of William Penn, features a remarkable program to demonstrate seventeenth-century foodways and recipes. The primary source for these seventeenth-century recipes is Gulielma Penn's handwritten "receipt" book. The recipes of William Penn's first wife are available today because Penn's son William had Edward Blackfan transcribe them before his departure to Pennsylvania. Gulielma included recipes for a "spinaige" tart (page 62), chicken fricassee (page 57), and portingall cake (page 86), which Pennsbury Manor has adapted for modern cooking and preserving.

The Pennsbury kitchen was a busy place. In order to extend the season in which fruits and vegetables could be served, preserving them with either sugar or vinegar was essential (see pippin preserves, page 88). The cooks preserved the harvests from the first produce in the spring through the last in the fall.

At least once a week, the bake oven was fired for an entire day of baking. The oven was preheated to a temperature hotter than what was desired so that bread, pies, and small cakes could all be baked as the oven's temperature decreased throughout the day. After two loads of bread were baked, the cooks baked meat pies, such as shreed pyes (page 61).

Dinner for William Penn was served between 2:00 and 4:00 in the afternoon and typically contained multiple courses. Servants prepared the table with the same number of deliberately creased table linens as courses and arranged the prepared dishes symmetrically on the table. After each course, the servants removed both the remaining food and one tablecloth.

Right: *Cooks prepare a meal in Pennsbury Manor's kitchen.* DAVID J. HEALY

Below: *The Great Hall at Pennsbury Manor was used for dining on special occasions.* DAVID J. HEALY

Spaghetti Sauce

1 pound ground beef

1 small can tomato paste

1 can water

2 tablespoons butter

oregano

onion salt

salt and pepper

grated cheese

Cook meat thoroughly in large skillet and drain any grease. Then add tomato paste and water. Add butter, lots of oregano, a little onion salt, some salt and pepper, and mix in. Sprinkle some grated cheese on top. Cook for about 10 minutes on high. Lower heat and simmer for about 15 minutes. Serve over cooked pasta. Makes 6 servings.

Pennsylvania Military Museum

Festive Pork Roast

2- to 3-pound boneless pork roast

salt and pepper

1 teaspoon rosemary

1 cup golden raisins

1³/₄ cups canned pineapple juice

3 tablespoons peach jelly

1 tablespoon ginger

1 tablespoon cornstarch

sliced pineapple

Cut a slit lengthwise through the center of the top of the roast (do not go all the way through). Spread open and rub with salt, pepper, and rosemary. Stuff with raisins. Pull roast together and tie with string. Wrap in aluminum foil. Poke several holes in foil. Place in roasting pan, and roast for 1¹/₂ hours in 350-degree oven. Combine juice, jelly, ginger, and cornstarch in small saucepan. Cook over low heat until thick. When roast is done, remove foil and return roast to pan. Cover with sauce. Roast for an additional 15 to 20 minutes. Garnish with sliced pineapple. Makes 6 to 8 servings.

The State Museum of Pennsylvania

PENNSYLVANIA HISTORICAL AND MUSEUM COMMISSION

Fregasy (Fricassee) of Chicken

3 skinned, boneless whole chicken breasts, split

2 tablespoons butter

1/2 pound sliced fresh mushrooms

1/2 cup chicken broth

1/2 cup white wine

1/2 teaspoon sage

1/2 teaspoon thyme

1/2 teaspoon marjoram

dash ground nutmeg

juice of 1/2 lemon

2 egg yolks

4 lemon slices (for garnish)

1 tablespoon chopped fresh parsley (for garnish)

Cut each chicken breast in four pieces. Sauté in butter for about 3 minutes. Add mushrooms and sauté. Add chicken broth, wine, and seasonings. Simmer 15 minutes uncovered. Add lemon juice. Beat egg yolks, and stir in a small amount of hot broth before adding the beaten yolks to the chicken mixture. Stir constantly over low heat until thickened, but do not boil. Garnish with 4 lemon slices and parsley. Serve over biscuits. Makes 6 servings.

Pennsbury Manor

African Vegetarian Stew

4 small kohlrabies or parsnips, peeled and cut into chunks

¹/₂ cup couscous or bulgur wheat

I large onion, chopped

¹/₄ cup raisins, dark or golden

2 sweet potatoes, peeled and cut into chunks

I teaspoon ground coriander

¹/₂ teaspoon ground turmeric

2 zucchini, sliced thick

¹/₂ teaspoon ground cinnamon

5 fresh or 16-ounce can tomatoes

¹/₂ teaspoon ground ginger

¹/₄ teaspoon ground cumin

15-ounce can garbanzo beans

3 cups water

Combine all ingredients in large saucepan. Bring to a boil, lower the heat, and simmer until vegetables are tender, about 30 minutes. Makes 8 servings. *Note:* Serve the couscous separately, if desired.

The State Museum of Pennsylvania

Bouille Beef

I beef rump

5 carrots

5 turnips

3 onions

2 celery ribs

2 bunches pot herbs

3 tablespoons mace

I tablespoon sweet marjoram

6 cloves

handful salt

¹/₂ teaspoon pepper

¹/₂ cup capers

Wash the rump of beef well, and tie it up. Put it into a pot, and nearly fill it with water. Add vegetables and seasonings. Begin cooking 8 hours before you plan to eat. Bring to a boil, then lower the heat so it simmers as slowly as possible. About $1/2$ hour before dinner, take out the gravy, strain, and skim off all the fat. Thicken with flour, bring to a boil, then remove from heat. Add capers and a little of the caper vinegar. Pour over the beef when ready for the table. Makes 6 to 8 servings.

Cornwall Iron Furnace

Swedish Meatballs

$1/2$ **cup unseasoned bread crumbs**

$1/2$ **cup half-and-half**

4 tablespoons unsalted butter, divided

$1/4$ **cup minced white onions**

$1/3$ **pound each ground beef, veal, and pork**

1 large egg

$1/8$ **teaspoon freshly grated nutmeg**

$1/2$ **teaspoon salt, or to taste**

$1/4$ **teaspoon freshly ground black pepper**

In large mixing bowl, soak bread crumbs in half-and-half for 5 minutes. Melt 1 tablespoon butter in small skillet over low to moderate heat. When foam starts to subside, add onions and sauté for about 2 minutes. Let cool slightly. Add meats, egg, nutmeg, salt, pepper, and cooked onions to the bread crumb mixture. Gently combine ingredients with your hands. Cover the bowl and refrigerate for a couple hours. Then shape the meat mixture with your hands into uniform $2/3$-inch balls. Arrange on plate or dish in one layer so they do not touch each other. Let them stand at room temperature for 30 minutes. Melt remaining butter in a sauté pan or skillet over moderate heat. When foam starts to subside, add meatballs. Do not crowd pan. Sauté meatballs for about 5 minutes, until they are brown on all sides. If you cook the meatballs in batches, keep the cooked ones warm in a preheated 200-degree oven. Serve on a warm platter. Makes 8 servings.

Morton Homestead

Vegetables and Sides

Sauerkraut

cabbage heads

salt

Halve or quarter the heads of cabbage. Using a shredder or sharp knife, cut the cabbage into thin shreds, about the thickness of a dime. Place in a large crock or glass container, and sprinkle some salt on it, more or less to suit your taste. Pack it down firmly with a stomper or your hand. Repeat shredding, salting, and stomping until juice comes to the surface. Keep repeating this process until container is almost full, about 4 inches from the top. Be sure, with each stomping, that juice always squishes over the shredded cabbage; the fermenting cabbage must not be exposed to air. Place a large enough plastic bag, partially filled with water, over the top. It should be watertight, and it must touch all the interior sides of the container to seal out the air. It also serves as a weight. Place the crock somewhere where the fermentation odor will not be annoying, such as a garage or cellar.

Ideal temperature is 68 to 72 degrees for fermentation, which takes about 6 to 8 weeks. Test by pulling a small portion of the bag away from the edge. If no bubbles appear or can be seen, it is finished. After fermentation, if brownness or discoloration is seen at the edges of the sauerkraut, spoon away the discolored portion and throw it away. This browning at the edges is normal. When fermentation is complete, heat sauerkraut to simmering. Then pack into clean, hot jars, and cover with hot juice to about 1 inch from top of jar. Close jars tightly, and process 20 minutes for pints or 30 minutes for quarts in a boiling water bath. Cool, test the seal, and store. Sauerkraut can also be taken from the crock and frozen in tightly sealed plastic containers.

Ephrata Cloister

Left: *Re-enactors make sauerkraut—a Pennsylvania German specialty—at Landis Valley Museum.* CRAIG A. BENNER

Corn Pie

piecrust

1 dozen ears fresh raw corn

2 potatoes, diced

2 to 4 hard-boiled eggs, sliced

green pepper, parsley, onion (optional)

butter or margarine

1 to 2 tablespoons flour

1 cup milk

This dish may be prepared with or without a bottom crust. If you make a pie without a bottom crust, grease deep pie dish with butter or margarine. Cut corn off cobs. Peel potatoes and cut into $1/2$- to $3/4$-inch cubes. Mix with corn. Slice hard-boiled eggs and mix with corn and potatoes. Add salt and pepper to taste. If desired, add chopped fresh green pepper, parsley, and/or onion (purists don't use anything but corn and eggs). Dot top of vegetables with butter or margarine. Sprinkle flour over vegetables. Pour on milk to a level almost to the top of the corn. Roll out pie pastry to fit top of dish. Place on top of vegetables and flute edges. Cut slits in top of crust to allow steam to escape. Bake in 425-degree preheated oven until crust is brown and milk is bubbling throughout, about 25 to 30 minutes. Makes 6 servings. *Note:* The corn will cook quickly, and so will other ingredients. Be sure the potato cubes are not too large, or they will not cook at the same rate as the corn. In all likelihood, this pie will boil over in the cooking process toward the end of the baking time. Be prepared by putting a sheet of foil on the second shelf halfway through the baking time.

Cornwall Iron Furnace

Stuffed Mushrooms

12 large mushrooms

6-ounce can fresh or frozen king crabmeat

1 can consommé

1 tablespoon grated Swiss or mozzarella cheese

Wash mushrooms and remove stems. Sauté caps until slightly brown. Mix crabmeat with consommé and salt. Place caps, hollow side up, in buttered baking dish and stuff with crabmeat mixture. Top with grated cheese. Bake 20 minutes at 350 degrees. Makes 2 servings.

Pennsylvania Military Museum

THE MILITARY MOVES
ON ITS STOMACH

During World War I, soldiers' rations contained more items than they had previously. Though lacking in vitamin A, the rations kept the soldiers relatively healthy, a difficult task in trench conditions. They were expensive, however, and exceeded the ration allowance. To combat the rising costs, new items such as bacon, lard, onions, canned tomatoes, and margarine were introduced at the end of the war.

By the time America entered World War II, rations were more standardized and environment based. There were rations designed for the individual and the detachment, for use in the field or in combat.

Two familiar rations introduced at that time were C and K rations. C rations consisted of six cans—three with a meat and a vegetable, and the other three with crackers, sugar, and coffee. Packed with 2,974 calories, C rations were considered too bulky for use by mobile troops. K rations, adopted in 1942, were created to meet the needs of paratroopers, tank crews, and other soldiers who depended on mobility for survival. Both kinds of rations remained in service for decades, feeding troops in Korea and Vietnam.

During World War II, Allied POWs in Europe, dubbed "Kriegies" by the Germans, received German rations supplemented by Red Cross packages and found creative ways to spice up their diet. "Kriegie ice cream" was prepared by beating snow with powdered milk and sugar until fluffed, then topping with jam. "Macaroni and cheese" consisted of broken-up crackers, milk, and sliced cheese heated together.

The Pennsylvania Military Museum, Boalsburg, Centre County, honors and tells the story of America's citizen soldiers.

Fried Potatoes

6 to 8 large potatoes
salt
2 tablespoons butter or bacon drippings
1 large onion, diced
1 3/4 cups beef broth
1/4 cup chopped parsley
1 cup bread crumbs
salt and pepper to taste
saffron

Wash and peel potatoes. Cut into bite-size pieces and salt them. Let potatoes stand for 30 minutes. Melt butter or bacon drippings in a frying pan, and add diced onion. Drain potatoes, and fry with onion until brown and tender. Make a sauce with the beef broth, parsley, and bread crumbs. Season with salt, pepper, and saffron. Pour sauce over potatoes before serving. Makes 10 to 12 servings.

Old Economy Village

CRAIG A. BENNER

German Potato Pancakes

4 cups grated raw potatoes
1/2 onion, minced
4 tablespoons flour
I teaspoon salt
2 eggs
shortening

Grate enough potatoes to make a heaping 4 cups; drain thoroughly in a colander. Combine potatoes with onion, flour, salt, and eggs. Mix thoroughly. Drop by large spoonfuls into a skillet containing 1/2 inch of hot vegetable shortening and cook about 4 minutes on each side, or until outside edges are crisp and centers are done. These also may be served as a main dish, accompanied by hot homemade applesauce, sour cream, or pancake syrup. Makes 6 servings.

Eckley Miners' Village

Swedish Potato Pancakes

2 cups milk, divided
2 eggs, beaten
1/2 cup flour
I teaspoon sugar
I teaspoon salt
freshly ground black pepper
1 1/3 cups grated potatoes
2 cups lingonberries or raspberries

Add 1/4 cup milk to eggs. Blend in flour. Add remaining milk, sugar, salt, and pepper. Beat until smooth. Let stand 2 hours. Squeeze grated potatoes dry and add to batter. Heat griddle and grease lightly. Use 1/4 cup batter for each pancake. Fold pancakes in quarters. Serve with berries. Makes 14 to 16 pancakes.

Morton Homestead

Dried String Beans with Ham

I pound dried string beans
ham end, ham hocks, or meaty ham bone
potatoes (optional)
dried lima or kidney beans (optional)

Soak beans overnight. Do not drain. Add ham and simmer for several hours, until beans are tender. Add more water, and season if not salty enough. A few potatoes can be added the last 1/2 hour of cooking, and dried lima or kidney beans are sometimes "put with." Makes 4 to 6 servings. *Note:* Fresh vegetables were available only in the summer. At other times, dried vegetables had to be used.

Graeme Park

Loksa

3 cups cooked, salted, well-mashed, and cooled potatoes
1/2 cup butter
1/2 cup flour

Blend butter and flour into mashed potatoes. The dough should not be too sticky or too crumbly—add a bit more flour if necessary. Divide dough into four portions and roll out each portion on a floured board to 1/8 inch thickness, forming circles about 8 inches in diameter. Prick surface with a fork to prevent puffing. Place on a preheated, buttered griddle on stovetop and cook like pancakes. Alternatively, place on a greased cookie sheet and bake in a preheated 400-degree oven for about 7 minutes on each side. Remove from griddle or oven and brush each side with butter; cut into wedges. Makes 6 servings.

Anthracite Heritage Museum
Eckley Miners' Village

Baked Corn Custard

16-ounce can cream-style corn
1/2 can milk
2 eggs
2 tablespoons margarine
2 tablespoons sugar

Pour creamed corn into baking dish, and add margarine. Fill empty can halfway with milk, and add eggs and sugar. With fork, beat milk, eggs, and sugar together, then pour into baking dish with creamed corn and margarine; stir to mix. Bake in 350-degree oven for 35 minutes. Or cook on high in microwave in 5-minute increments, loosening solids from edge of dish and carefully moving to middle, bringing liquid to sides of dish. Usually takes 15 to 20 minutes to cook completely in microwave. Makes 4 servings.

Fort Pitt Museum

Serving loksa at Eckley Miners' Village. CRAIG A. BENNER

Baked Beans

I pound dried navy or pea beans
¹/₂ pound salt pork, without rind
I medium onion, sliced
¹/₄ cup dark brown sugar, packed
3 tablespoons molasses
I teaspoon salt
¹/₄ teaspoon dry mustard
¹/₈ teaspoon pepper
4 to 6 strips cooked bacon, crumbled

Place beans in large saucepan and cover with water. Heat to boiling, and boil 2 minutes. Remove from heat and let stand for 1 hour. Add water if necessary to cover beans. Simmer uncovered 50 minutes, or until tender; do not boil or the beans will burst. Drain beans, reserving liquid. Heat oven to 300 degrees. Cut salt pork into several pieces; layer with beans and onion in 2-quart ungreased beanpot or casserole. Stir together remaining ingredients and 1 cup of reserved liquid; pour over beans. Add enough of the remaining reserved liquid or water to almost cover beans. Cover and bake for 3¹/₂ to 4 hours. Remove cover for last half of baking time. If beans look dry during baking, stir to mix. Serves 6 to 8.

Pennsylvania Lumber Museum

German Potato Salad

4 strips of bacon
I small onion, minced
6 red potatoes
¹/₂ cup cider vinegar
¹/₄ cup water
I teaspoon sugar
I teaspoon dry mustard
¹/₂ teaspoon celery seed

Cook bacon over slow heat until very crisp. Remove with a slotted spoon and set aside. Sauté onion in remaining bacon fat until golden. Keep warm. Meanwhile, boil potatoes in enough water to cover until barely tender. Peel and slice while warm. In a small saucepan, boil together vinegar, water, sugar, mustard, and celery seed until sugar is dissolved. Combine with onion, then add potatoes. Sprinkle with crumbled bacon. Serve warm. Makes 4 to 6 servings.

Museum of Anthracite Mining

Scalloped Potatoes

2 pounds potatoes, about 6 medium
$1/4$ cup finely chopped onion
3 tablespoons flour
I teaspoon salt
$1/4$ teaspoon pepper
$1/4$ cup butter or margarine
$2^1/2$ cups milk

Wash potatoes; pare thinly and remove eyes. Cut potatoes into thin slices to measure about 4 cups. In greased 2-quart casserole, arrange potatoes in four layers, sprinkling each of the first three with 1 tablespoon onion, 1 tablespoon flour, $1/4$ teaspoon salt, and dash pepper, and dotting each with 1 tablespoon butter. Sprinkle top with remaining onion, salt, and pepper, and dot with remaining butter. Heat milk just to scalding; pour over potatoes. Cover; bake at 350 degrees for 30 minutes. Uncover; bake 60 to 70 minutes longer, or until potatoes are tender. Let stand 5 to 10 minutes before serving. Makes 8 servings.

Drake Well Museum

Asparagus

I pound asparagus
I teaspoon salt
I tablespoon sugar
I lemon, cut in half crosswise
I tablespoon butter
2 tablespoons flour
2 egg yolks
nutmeg
salt and pepper to taste

Clean asparagus and cut into 1-inch pieces. Put in pot and cover with water. Add salt, sugar, and $1/2$ lemon cut into slices, and simmer until asparagus is tender. Drain water, reserving 1 to $1^1/2$ cups for sauce. Cream butter, and add flour, egg yolks, and asparagus water. Squeeze juice from remaining $1/2$ lemon and add to sauce. Minced lemon peel may also be added. Cook over low heat until bubbly. Pour sauce over asparagus and sprinkle with nutmeg. Season with salt and pepper as needed. Makes 6 servings.

Old Economy Village

DINING ON THE RAILROAD

When the first passenger train pulled out of Charleston, South Carolina, in 1830, an immediate problem was created: how to feed travelers en route. American enterprise initially filled the need in a haphazard way. When trains pulled into towns, vendors would offer food—chicken, hard-boiled eggs, hams, pies, cakes, custards, coffee, fresh fruit from local orchards, peanuts, soft drinks, and even ice cream—to passengers leaning out train windows, or the vendors would board the train until it departed. The scene at the train station was chaotic, and the food ranged from bad tasting to rancid. Some passengers packed baskets of food, but the result was sometimes equally bad. As one reporter wrote, "The bouquet from those lunches hung around the car all day and the flies wired ahead for their friends to meet them at each station."

The railroad owners soon realized they could earn additional revenue by building or licensing restaurants along the train routes. But even this improvement was problematic for passengers, who might have no more than twenty or thirty minutes at a station to eat and get back on the train. Pandemonium ensued as crowds rushed from the train, jostled each other to get served, then rushed back to the train before it departed. And often the train schedule necessitated inconvenient meal times. Passengers often labeled the eating house an "indigestion house."

The key seemed to be feeding the passengers on the train, which was convenient for the passengers and more profitable for the railroads. The first dining car, a remodeled day coach, appeared on the Philadelphia, Wilmington, and Baltimore Railroad in 1862. Soon competitive pressure forced other railroads to add dining cars. The appeal of the separate dining car was further enhanced when the Pennsylvania Railroad (PRR) in 1887 became the first to offer a vestibule, a flexible covered connection that allowed passengers to move safely and comfortably between cars.

By 1927, the dining car had become a routine part of passenger rail service. The Pennsylvania Railroad Dining Car School was opened that year to teach "deft and courteous service," as well as the proper preparation of meat, soup stock, salads,

PENNSYLVANIA HISTORICAL AND MUSEUM COMMISSION

Chefs prepare desserts for passengers of the Pennsylvania Railroad. PENNSYLVANIA STATE ARCHIVES

relishes, breads, desserts, and beverages. The PRR Dining Car Department put out a 109-page booklet of cooking instructions for the preparation of dishes served in the railroad's dining cars. It was not unusual for the well-designed kitchens in the dining cars to serve 300 or more meals a day. By 1938, the PRR was serving 3,000,000 meals a year in its dining cars, with patrons annually consuming 2,500,000 eggs, 550,000 pounds of fowl, 390,999 pounds of beef, 490,000 pounds of pork products, 300,000 pounds of fish, 1,000,000 pounds of potatoes, 350,000 heads of lettuce, 1,300,000 oranges, and 2,000,000 cups of coffee.

Perhaps the most memorable aspects of a dining-car meal were the impeccable service and the ambience, with neat linen tablecloths and napkins, patterned china, silver place settings, and stylish tables and chairs. Passengers could take in the scenery while enjoying a sumptuous meal served by courteous waiters and prepared by skilled chefs in a dining car with the atmosphere of a five-star hotel. A typical dinner menu on the PRR might have included Pennsylvania Dutch chicken, baked potato Pennsylvania (page 78), corn and green pepper sauté, cream of chicken soup, Roquefort cheese, deviled slice of roast beef with mustard sauce, ginger muffins, melon mint cocktail, baked Indian pudding (page 82), Pennepicure pie (a rich raisin custard pie topped with meringue), salad with Pennsylvania dressing, stuffed celery, and veal cutlets in paprika sauce.

By 1949, 170 dining cars were in operation on the PRR alone, serving more than 4,400,000 meals. Railroad travel declined after World War II, however, and though the PRR invested more than $4,000,000 in coffee shop lounge cars and modernizing the dining cars, the golden age of railroad dining was fast disappearing.

At the Railroad Museum of Pennsylvania in Strasburg, Lancaster County, you can see original dining cars and learn more about the state's rich railroad heritage.

Traveling and dining in style, 1925.
RAILROAD MUSEUM OF PENNSYLVANIA

The Pennsylvania Railroad's wartime menu, 1942.
RAILROAD MUSEUM OF PENNSYLVANIA

Baked Potato Pennsylvania

2 cups boiled new potatoes, mashed
4 Idaho baking potatoes
1 1/2 cups light cream
2 ounces butter
salt and pepper to taste
toppings: bread crumbs, grated Parmesan cheese, paprika, melted butter

Place 4 or 5 medium new potatoes in medium saucepan, cover with salted water, and bring to a boil. Cover and cook for 25 minutes. Drain and let stand to cool to room temperature. Meanwhile, bake Idaho potatoes well, about 1 hour in 350-degree oven. Cool baked potatoes and cut tops off lengthwise. Scoop out potato pulp until shell is well hollowed out. Now remove skins from boiled new potatoes, place in medium saucepan, and mash thoroughly. Add cream and butter to mashed boiled new potatoes, mixing well. Season to taste and cook over medium heat for about 10 minutes, until butter melts and mixture is bubbly. Place hollowed-out potato shells in baking dish and fill each with potato mixture. Sprinkle tops with bread crumbs, grated cheese, pinches of paprika, and a few drops of melted butter. Bake until golden brown. Serve very hot. Makes 4 servings.

The Pennsylvania Railroad offered these variations:

- Instead of using new potatoes, mash baked potato pulp with salt, pepper, 2 tablespoons butter, 1 heaping teaspoon each chopped parsley and chopped chives, and 1/3 cup light cream, then refill the shells, sprinkle with melted butter, and brown in the oven.
- Follow the above variation, but substitute 2/3 cup shredded cheese for chopped parsley and chives, and sprinkle top with additional shredded cheese.
- Mash the baked potato pulp with 4 tablespoons butter, 2 ounces Roquefort or bleu cheese, 2 tablespoons hot light cream, and a dash of salt and paprika. Return mixture to shells, and bake until the tops brown.

Railroad Museum of Pennsylvania

Colcannon

6 to 8 potatoes, boiled
1/2 to 3/4 cup milk or cream
1 cabbage, boiled
4 tablespoons butter
salt and pepper to taste
1/2 cup grated cheddar or other hard cheese (optional)
2 tablespoons butter (optional)

Coal companies sponsored competitions for the best vegetable garden in the mining community. PENNSYLVANIA STATE ARCHIVES

Mash potatoes with milk. Mince cabbage. Melt 4 tablespoons butter in saucepan. Put in potatoes and cabbage, and add salt and pepper to taste. Mix well. Serve when thoroughly hot. Or the mixture may be turned into a greased pie dish, sprinkled with grated cheese, dotted with an additional 2 tablespoons butter, and baked in a 350-degree oven until cheese is browned. Makes 8 to 10 servings.

Graeme Park

German Style Red Cabbage

2 tablespoons butter or margarine

1 small onion, chopped

3 tablespoons sugar, divided

6 cups red cabbage, shredded

¹/₂ cup red wine vinegar

1 ¹/₂ teaspoons salt

1 cup tart apple, peeled and diced

1 cup sour cream

In butter or margarine melted in a heavy skillet, cook onion until golden; sprinkle with 1 tablespoon sugar. Add cabbage, vinegar, and salt; cover and simmer gently for 15 minutes. Add apple and 2 tablespoons sugar; continue to cook 5 to 10 minutes longer. Meanwhile, bring sour cream to room temperature. Place cooked cabbage in serving dish, and spread sour cream over the top. Makes 8 servings.

Museum of Anthracite Mining

Desserts

Grandmother Fortney's Sand Tarts

2 cups sugar

10 ounces butter

2 eggs (reserve small amount of egg white mixed with a little water)

2²/₃ cups flour

almonds

nutmeg

cinnamon

Cream sugar and butter. Beat eggs into mixture. Add flour. Form into rolls about 1¹/₂ inches in diameter. Wrap in waxed paper and refrigerate overnight. Then slice into rounds and place on cookie sheet. Brush with egg white and water mix. Decorate with an almond half and shake on nutmeg or cinnamon. Bake at 350 degrees for 10 minutes. Makes 45 cookies. *Note:* Mrs. Fortney and her husband had a furniture store in Titusville until 1912.

Drake Well Museum

Lothians (Barley Pudding)

8 ounces barley

pinch salt

1 quart water

4 ounces currants

Put barley into pan with cold salted water and bring slowly to a boil. Cook for 1¹/₂ hours. Add washed currants and simmer for 1¹/₂ hours longer. Serve with sugar and thin cream or milk. Makes 4 to 6 servings.

Graeme Park

Left: *Making apple pies at Landis Valley Museum.* CRAIG A. BENNER

Concord Grape Pie

4 cups Concord grapes
I cup sugar
¹/₈ teaspoon salt
3 tablespoons flour or 2¹/₂ tablespoons minute tapioca
pastry for 9-inch double crust
I tablespoon lemon juice
I tablespoon butter or margarine

Skin grapes, saving skins, and put pulp in saucepan without water. Bring to boil. While hot, put through strainer to remove seeds. Combine strained pulp with skins. Mix sugar, salt, and flour or tapioca together. Put about ¹/₄ of this mixture on bottom of piecrust, and mix remainder with grapes. Add lemon juice. Turn into crust and dot with butter. Cover with top crust, and bake at 450 degrees for 10 minutes, then reduce heat to 350 degrees and bake for 25 to 30 minutes longer.

Drake Well Museum

Indian Pudding

¹/₂ cup cornmeal
4 cups whole milk, hot
¹/₂ cup maple syrup
¹/₄ cup light molasses
2 eggs, slightly beaten
2 tablespoons melted butter or margarine
¹/₃ cup brown sugar, packed
I teaspoon salt
¹/₄ teaspoon cinnamon
³/₄ teaspoon ginger
¹/₂ cup whole milk, cold

In top of double boiler, slowly stir cornmeal into hot milk and cook over boiling water, stirring occasionally, about 20 minutes. Lightly grease 2-quart baking dish (8¹/₂ inches round). In small bowl, combine rest of ingredients, except cold milk. Stir into cornmeal mixture and mix well. Turn into prepared dish; pour cold milk on top without stirring. Bake at 300 degrees uncovered for 2 hours, or just until set but quivery. Do not overbake. Let stand for 30 minutes before serving. Serve with vanilla ice cream or light cream. Makes 10 to 12 servings.

Conrad Weiser Homestead

NATIVE AMERICAN FOODWAYS

William Penn was a friend of the native Lenape who were inhabitants of his new colony of Pennsylvania. The foodways of the Lenape were curiously different, and Penn had a thirst for knowledge about all the ways and customs of these people. For the English, wheat was the most important grain; for the Lenape, it was corn. Besides corn, they cultivated beans and squash. They also foraged for many other plants, including Jerusalem artichokes and sunflowers.

Penn and the colonists learned from Pennsylvania's native peoples about these indigenous foods, which became a staple of American and Pennsylvania cooking. The gardens at Pennsbury Manor in Morrisville, Bucks County, incorporated both traditional English garden elements and the plants adopted from Native Americans— corn, squash, sunflowers (see sunflower seed cakes, page 90), and medicinal plants.

The Conrad Weiser Homestead, in Womelsdorf, Berks County, celebrates the life of the man who is credited with maintaining peace with the powerful Iroquois Confederacy. Conrad Weiser's career as an interpreter and negotiator with the Native Americans began in 1731 and resulted in a close relationship built on mutual trust. Weiser had a more intimate relationship with Native Americans than almost any other colonist. He walked their trails, ate their foods, spoke their language, and slept in their longhouses.

In the summer of 1744, Weiser traveled to Lancaster to negotiate a treaty with the Indians. The Iroquois Confederacy sent a delegation of 252, and 24 other chiefs attended, as well as leaders from Penn's colony and commissioners from Maryland and Virginia. After exchanging gifts, a banquet was served, and the subsequent talks resulted in the Lancaster Treaty. There are no records of the menu, but it may have included foods familiar to the Native Americans in attendance, such as Indian pudding (page 82) and acorn squash soup (page 17).

An early, though somewhat fanciful, depiction of a Pennsylvania Susquehannock Indian village with agricultural pursuits and livestock. PENNSYLVANIA HISTORICAL AND MUSEUM COMMISSION

Shoo Fly Pie

1 cup brown sugar

1 cup molasses

1 egg

1 teaspoon baking soda

1 tablespoon flour

2 cups boiling water

9-inch unbaked piecrust

Mix together first five ingredients. Add boiling water, then chill for about 1 hour. Pour into piecrust.

Crumbs

2 cups flour

1 cup brown sugar

1 teaspoon baking powder

pinch salt

1/2 cup shortening

Combine dry ingredients, and then cut in shortening. Top pie with crumb mixture. Bake at 375 degrees for about 35 minutes.

Cornwall Iron Furnace

Lehigh Valley Baked Apple Dish

4 cups sugar

6 large Rome Beauty apples

3 maraschino cherries

Spread sugar in bottom of baking pan. Core apples, and cut 1/4 inch from top of each so that apples can rest upside down on bottom of pan on sugar. Place apples in this position. Sprinkle water lightly along the edge of the baking pan to keep sugar from burning. Place baking dish in 300-degree oven, and bake until apples are fork-tender, about 1 hour. Baste occasionally as sugar forms syrup to coat each apple with a glaze. After apples become thoroughly glazed, turn them over and place half a maraschino cherry in center of each. Continue to baste until cooked through, about 15 minutes more. Serve hot. Makes 6 servings. *Note:* This was a popular dessert on the Lehigh Valley Railroad.

Railroad Museum of Pennsylvania

Popcorn Balls

popcorn, about 4 quarts popped

2 cups molasses

I cup brown sugar

I tablespoon vinegar

butter (size of small egg)

Make the candy in a large kettle. Pop the corn, salt it, and sift it through the fingers so that the extra salt and unpopped kernels drop through. Stir the popcorn into the kettle, then heap it on buttered plates or make it into balls. Makes 10 to 12 popcorn balls.

Eckley Miners' Village

Pineapple Squares

2^1/$_2$ cups crushed pineapple (I pound, 4 ounces)

^{1}/$_2$ cup sugar

^{1}/$_2$ cup water

2 tablespoons cornstarch

Mix the above ingredients together and cook over low heat until thick. Cool.

Dough

3 cups flour

I teaspoon baking soda

^{1}/$_2$ cup sugar

^{1}/$_2$ pound margarine

^{1}/$_2$ cup sour cream

I teaspoon vanilla

2 egg yolks

^{1}/$_2$ cup crushed nuts

Mix dough ingredients together then divide dough into two parts. Roll one part for the bottom on a sheet of waxed paper, and place in a jelly roll pan. Spread pineapple filling over bottom dough. Roll out the other part and place over the top. Sprinkle top with nuts. Bake at 350 to 375 degrees for 30 minutes. Cut into squares when cooled. Makes 25 squares.

Cornwall Iron Furnace

Portingall Cakes

1 1/4 cups sugar, divided
2 cups flour
1/2 pound butter
1 tablespoon rose water
2 eggs plus 1 egg yolk
1 cup currants
1/3 cup water

Combine 1 cup sugar and flour in bowl. Cream butter in separate bowl. Add half of sugar and flour mixture to butter. Add rose water. Add eggs plus egg yolk. Add remaining half of sugar and flour mixture. Mix well. The dough will be thick. Add currants. Mix 1/4 cup sugar and water, and heat in a small pan to make syrup. Fill cupcake pans 3/4 full with dough, and pour a small amount of syrup over each cake. Bake at 350 degrees for 20 minutes. Makes about 3 dozen cakes.

Pennsbury Manor

Rhubarb Bread Pudding

2 cups diced rhubarb
2 cups freshly sliced strawberries
1 1/2 cups sugar
2 teaspoons grated lemon rind
2 cups scalded milk
2 eggs
1 tablespoon vanilla
4 cups bread cubes
1/4 cup butter

Butter a 12x9x2-inch baking dish. Mix rhubarb, strawberries, sugar, and lemon rind together. Set aside. Slowly add eggs and vanilla to milk. Mix milk mixture with bread cubes. Add the fruit mixture and stir lightly. Pour into baking dish. Dot with butter. Bake at 375 degrees for 1 hour. Makes 4 to 6 servings.

Drake Well Museum

Hard Times Cake

2 cups sugar

2 cups water

I pound raisins, chopped

1/4 cup lard

3 cups flour, sifted

I teaspoon salt

2 teaspoons cinnamon

2 teaspoons ground cloves

2 teaspoons baking soda

Simmer together sugar, water, raisins, and lard for 5 minutes; set aside
to cool. Sift together dry ingredients; add to raisin mixture and beat until
smooth. Pour into two greased and floured 9x5-inch loaf pans. Bake in 325-
degree oven for 1 hour and 30 minutes, or until done. Makes 2 loaves. *Note:*
This cake was baked when eggs, milk, and butter were scarce. It was also called
economy cake, poverty cake, poor man's cake, or mother's minus cake.

Museum of Anthracite Mining

Chees (Cheese) Cake

pastry dough, cut into 4-inch circles

I pound softened cream cheese

1/2 cup softened butter

1/4 cup sugar

dash nutmeg

I teaspoon rose water

3 egg yolks

1/2 cup cream

1/2 cup currants

Line tart shells or muffin tins with pastry dough. Dough should not be too
thin and does not have to reach top of pan. Mix cream cheese, butter, sugar,
nutmeg, rose water, egg yolks, and cream with electric mixer, food processor,
or by hand. Add currants. Pour mixture into crust-lined pans, filling just to
top of pastry. Bake at 350 degrees for 20 to 25 minutes. Remove from oven
and cool completely in pan. Makes 4 small cakes. *Note:* This recipe was
adapted from Gulielma Penn's seventeenth-century recipe (receipt) book.

Pennsbury Manor

Apple Dumplings

12 cups flour

1 1/2 tablespoons salt

4 1/2 tablespoons sugar

4 cups shortening

1 cup cold water

18 baking/cooking apples

1 cup Karo syrup

1 cup water

1/4 pound butter

2 tablespoons cinnamon

3/4 cup sugar

To make pastry, mix flour, salt, and sugar, then cut in shortening. Add water a little at a time to make a firm pastry dough. Core and peel apples. Prepare simple syrup by heating Karo and water in small pan. Cut butter into about 18 slices. Mix cinnamon and sugar. Roll out dough to 1/8 inch thickness. Cut into 18 5-to-7-inch squares. Place one prepared apple in middle of each dough square. Put 1/2 slice butter (about 1/2 tablespoon) in cavity where core was removed, and fill remaining space with cinnamon sugar. Wrap dough around apple, and place in baking dish. Take simple syrup and add liberally, drizzling dumplings and covering base of baking pan to a depth of about 1/4 inch. Bake at 400 degrees for 10 minutes. Reduce temperature to 350 degrees and continue baking for about 30 minutes more. Test apples for doneness. Makes 18 dumplings. *Note:* These dumplings are from the Cloister's annual apple dumpling sale in October.

Ephrata Cloister

Pippin (Apple) Preserves

1 1/2 cups sugar

1/2 cup water

1/2 cup white wine

1 pound apples (3 to 4)

Mix sugar, water, and wine in a frying pan or large pot big enough for apples to be in one layer. Heat on low until sugar is dissolved. Add apples that have been peeled and cut in eighths. Simmer on low heat until just soft. Cool apples in syrup and refrigerate. Makes 6 servings. *Note:* This recipe, from William Penn's wife, Gulielma, makes a nice accompaniment to pork.

Pennsbury Manor

DISAPPEARING FOODS

As Pennsylvania has grown and prospered over the centuries, many foods have disappeared from the commonwealth's tables. Squirrel, groundhog, pigeon, and rabbit—just another meal on the Pennsylvania frontier—are rarely served today. And few menus feature dandelion greens; pemmican, dried meat mixed with animal fat and berries; samp, a corn porridge; or skillygallee, fried pork and crumbled hardtack. Homemade root beer (page 116) is a rare treat.

Pioneer cooks found innovative solutions when certain ingredients were not available or their importation was too expensive. For example, early immigrants enjoyed pickled foods but did not have the necessary ingredients, such as vinegar, to make them. Then they discovered pickleweed, or picklewort, growing along the brackish marsh areas of the Delaware River. This succulent, salt-loving plant tastes like pickles and is an excellent source of iodine. Though most people today are not familiar with pickleweed, it was well known to many Colonial cooks.

At Lancaster County's Landis Valley Museum, the largest museum in the United States of early Pennsylvania Dutch life, including foodways, the nationally recognized Heirloom Seed Project is working to keep plants with historical significance from extinction. Volunteers assist experts in researching, testing, and preserving more than 200 varieties of herbs, vegetables, and ornamental plants used by the Pennsylvania Dutch between 1750 and 1940, such as Deacon Dan beets, Seneca corn, Riesentraube tomatoes, and flax. Because these plants have not been hybridized, gardeners can save seeds from heirloom varieties with the assurance that each new generation of plants will bear fruit that is similar to the fruit from past seasons. The Heirloom Seed Project also offers seeds, techniques, and growing information to the public. Heirloom varieties of plants are for sale during the Herb and Garden Faire in mid-May.

PENNSYLVANIA STATE ARCHIVES

Sunflower Seed Cakes

3 cups shelled sunflower seeds
3 cups water
6 tablespoons cornmeal
fat for frying

Place sunflower seeds in water, and simmer until soft enough to mash, adding water during cooking if necessary. Drain off water and reserve. Place cooked seeds in food processor or blender until well mashed. Add cornmeal, and mix with mashed seeds to make a dough. Form into 2-inch-round flat cakes. Add some of the reserved liquid if dough gets too dry. Heat frying pan or griddle and melt fat. When fat is hot, fry cakes until golden and crusty on both sides. May be served with maple syrup. Makes 8 to 10 cakes.

Pennsbury Manor

Black Walnut Cake

3 cups flour
1³/₄ cups sugar
2 teaspoons baking powder
1¹/₂ teaspoons salt
4 eggs, divided
1 cup shortening
³/₄ cup milk
2 teaspoons vanilla
1 cup black walnuts, chopped

Shortening, eggs, and milk should be at room temperature. Sift together flour, sugar, baking powder, and salt. Add 2 eggs, shortening, milk, and vanilla to flour mixture, and beat for 2 minutes. Add 2 remaining eggs and beat an additional 2 minutes. Fold in black walnuts. Pour batter into bundt-type baking pan. Bake at 375 degrees for 1 hour. When cool, remove from pan and glaze the cake.

Glaze

2 tablespoons Karo syrup
2 tablespoons butter

Combine Karo and butter in saucepan. Bring to a boil, and boil 2 minutes. Pour over cake.

Joseph Priestley House

Welsh Currant Cookies

3 1/2 cups flour

1 cup sugar

1 teaspoon salt

3 teaspoons baking powder

1 1/2 teaspoons nutmeg

3/4 cup dried currants

1 cup shortening

2 unbeaten eggs

1/2 cup milk

Combine dry ingredients. Cut in shortening with pastry blender or knives until mixture is crumbly as pie dough. Add eggs and milk, and mix all together. Roll 1/8 inch thick, and cut with cookie cutter, biscuit cutter, or rim of glass. Heat griddle and cook 5 minutes on each side, or bake in preheated oven at 375 degrees for 10 to 12 minutes. Done when lightly browned. Makes 6 dozen cookies.

Joseph Priestley House

Mince Meat for Pies

3 pounds boiled beef or beef tongue

3 pounds raisins

3 pounds currants

3 pounds beef suet

3 lemons

3 pounds brown sugar

1 1/2 pounds citron

8 medium or 10 small apples

1 pint wine

1 pint brandy

3 ounces cinnamon

3 ounces cloves

3 ounces allspice

1 ounce grated nutmeg

Chop each item fine, separately, then mix all ingredients together well. It is best to leave out a small portion of the wine and brandy until you have tried the mince. If you find it too dry, a little cider may be added to the pies before baking. *Note:* This will make enough filling for 20 pies. Can be frozen in 1-pie portions for later use.

Cornwall Iron Furnace

Solstice Twelfth-Day Cake

Saturnalia and other ancient solstice-related festivals were ruled by a "king for a day." People voted for this pretend king using beans as counters. This custom changed and was adopted in another form by Christians. On the last night of the twelve days of Christmas, a cake was baked containing one dried bean for the king and one dried pea for the queen. If a man gets the slice of cake with the bean, he is the king. If a female gets it, she gets to pick the king. If a woman gets the pea, she is the queen, but if a man gets it, he picks the queen.

¹/₂ cup rum or fruit juice
I cup golden raisins
I cup golden currants
I cup seedless dark raisins
2 sticks unsalted butter, softened to room temperature
I cup sugar
4 large eggs
¹/₂ teaspoon cinnamon
¹/₄ teaspoon nutmeg
¹/₄ teaspoon mace
grated rind of I lemon
I dried pea
I dried bean
¹/₂ cup blanched almonds, roughly chopped
3 cups flour

In a bowl, combine rum or juice with raisins and currants. Let stand for several hours. Drain fruit, reserving the liquid. Preheat oven to 275 degrees. Grease a 10-inch cake pan that is at least 3 inches deep with butter or shortening. Line with baking parchment, if available. Cream butter and sugar together until light and fluffy. Beat in eggs one at a time until light and frothy. Beat in 3 tablespoons of the reserved liquid, and stir in spices and lemon rind. Stir in the pea and the bean. Stir in almonds and flour and mix well to make a smooth batter. Spoon batter into prepared cake pan and bake at 275 degrees for about 2 hours, or until cake tester comes out clean. Let cool in cake pan until just warm. Turn cake out onto cooling rack and peel away baking parchment.

Fancy Icing

2 egg whites, room temperature
pinch salt
2 cups confectioner's sugar
I tablespoon lemon juice

Beat egg whites with salt until very frothy. Beat in sugar and lemon juice until stiff peaks form. Add more sugar if needed to make a stiff paste. When cake is completely cool, spread top with icing.

Joseph Priestley House

Schnitz (Dried Apple) Pie

3 heaping cups dried apples (schnitz)
apple cider
double piecrust
$^1/_2$ teaspoon cinnamon

The night before, place dried apples in a crock, and add enough apple cider to cover. Next day, drain the apples (but enjoy the cider), and place apple slices in bottom piecrust. Sprinkle with cinnamon. Cover with top piecrust and crimp edges. Bake at 425 degrees for 15 minutes, then at 350 degrees for 30 minutes. *Note:* Unless you like a very sweet pie, the apples and cider usually provide enough sweetness.

Daniel Boone Homestead

Pound Cake

1 pound butter
1 pound sugar (4 cups)
1 pound flour (4 cups)
8 eggs
1 tablespoon cinnamon
$^1/_2$ nutmeg, grated
$^1/_2$ cup each brandy, wine, and rose water

Beat butter and sugar until creamy. Lightly beat eggs, then add alternately with flour, a little at a time. Add spices, then the other ingredients. Grease a sheet of baking parchment and put it in cake or bundt pan. Pour in cake batter, then put another sheet of paper over it. Bake at 325 degrees for 1 to $1^1/_2$ hours.

Icing

2 egg whites
4 cups confectioner's sugar

Beat egg whites till they fill a pint bowl, then mix in confectioner's sugar. Spread over cooled cake.

Cornwall Iron Furnace

Mrs. Evans Nut Horns

¹/₃ cake yeast
I cup cold water
6 cups flour
2 cups shortening
6 egg yolks, slightly beaten
pinch salt
sugar for rolling

Dissolve yeast in bowl with cold water. Add flour, shortening, egg yolks, and salt. Mix well. Knead until dough forms a smooth ball. Loosely wrap in plastic wrap and refrigerate for 2 hours. Roll out thin on white sugar, then cut into 3-inch squares.

Filling

4 to 6 cups walnuts, finely ground
³/₄ cup sugar
I teaspoon cinnamon
milk

Mix nuts, sugar, and cinnamon together, and add enough milk to moisten. Put teaspoonful of nut mixture in center of each pastry square. Roll corner to corner. Grease cookie sheet once. Bake at 350 degrees until lightly brown. Makes 10 to 11 dozen.

Pennsylvania Military Museum

Mrs. Degn's Ginger Snaps

I quart molasses
I pound sugar
I pound butter
3 pounds flour
4 tablespoons ginger
I teaspoon baking soda, dissolved in ¹/₄ cup water

Melt sugar in molasses, then stir in melted butter. Sift flour and ginger together, and add soda water. Mix all ingredients together thoroughly. Roll very thin and cut with a cookie cutter. Bake in a 350-degree oven for 10 to 12 minutes. Makes 10 dozen cookies.

Hope Lodge

THE HOMEFRONT
DURING WORLD WAR II

The hardships of a country at war hit the homefront during World War II. Shortages and rationing made the preparation of appealing and nutritious meals a real challenge. The traditional American meal of a meat dish, salad, and side dishes of vegetables and potatoes was limited by rationing. Recommendations of nonrationed foods that contained large amounts of important nutrients and vitamins were included in a variety of books and pamphlets designed to assist the homefront cook. Many labels on food were changed during the war, and cooks were encouraged to read the labels to make sure ingredients were all healthy and filled some nutritional requirement. Red meat, which was rationed, had to be replaced with other sources of protein. Poultry provided a good alternative for cooks, in part because it was more readily available—it could not be shipped to troops because it did not keep as long as beef. Fish was another great alternative to meat and also replaced meat in many meals. Cooks often fixed dishes using scraps that otherwise would have been thrown out. Peanuts and soybeans were substituted for meats, cheese became more popular, and eggs were included in many meals.

Fruits and vegetables were also in short supply. Families planted victory gardens, which provided more than half of all the vegetables in their diet, as well as fruits and even flowers.

Sugar, a crucial staple in American cooking, was rationed. Creative cooks found new ways to prepare old favorites by using honey or syrup to replace granulated sugar, as well as fruits from their gardens to sweeten dishes.

Cooks tried their hardest to make healthy and tasty meals despite shortages. Cooking on the homefront may have posed challenges, but cooks became more creative and resourceful because of the war.

(continued on page 96)

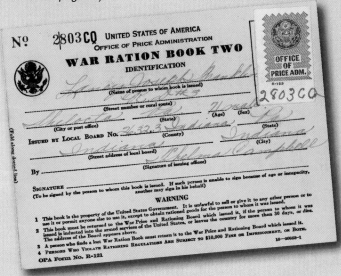

War ration book identification card, c. 1942. PENNSYLVANIA STATE ARCHIVES

Colorful wartime posters encouraged the public to grow their own produce and eat nutritiously. PENNSYLVANIA STATE ARCHIVES

(continued from page 95)
　　The Pennsylvania State Archives in Harrisburg, Dauphin County, contains wartime records from the Works Progress Administration, including posters, recipes, and instructional books. The Pennsylvania Military Museum in Boalsburg, Centre County, honors Pennsylvania's citizen soldiers.

Three-in-One Cookies

3/4 **cup butter**

2 **cups light brown sugar**

3 **eggs**

3 1/2 **cups flour**

3 **teaspoons baking powder**

1/2 **teaspoon salt**

3/4 **cup milk**

2 **teaspoons vanilla extract**

1 **teaspoon allspice**

1/2 **cup raisins**

2 **ounces unsweetened chocolate, melted**

1/2 **cup grated coconut**

Cream butter. Add sugar, and cream together thoroughly. Add eggs one at a time, beating well after each addition. Sift flour, measure, add baking powder and salt, and sift together. Add flour to first mixture alternately with milk. Add vanilla extract. Mix to a smooth, stiff dough. Divide into thirds and place in separate bowls. Add allspice and raisins to one bowl of dough, chocolate to second bowl, and coconut to third bowl. Mix each bowl well, and drop spoonfuls of dough on greased baking sheet. Bake in a 400-degree oven for 12 to15 minutes. Makes 3 dozen cookies. *Note:* Made by Mrs. Degn, last private owner of Hope Lodge.

Hope Lodge

Burnt Sugar Cake

1/2 **cup shortening**

1 1/2 **cups granulated sugar**

2 **eggs**

1 **cup milk**

3 **tablespoons burnt sugar syrup (see below)**

1 **teaspoon vanilla**

2 1/2 **cups flour**

2 **teaspoons baking powder**

Cream shortening and sugar. Add eggs and beat until creamy. Add next five ingredients in order. Bake at 350 degrees for 30 to 35 minutes.

Burnt Sugar Syrup

2/3 **cup maple sugar**

2/3 **cup boiling water**

In a heavy skillet, melt maple sugar over low heat, stirring constantly. When it is a dark brown, remove from heat. Slowly add boiling water. Heat and stir until well dissolved. Boil to reduce syrup to 1 cup. *Note:* An alternative is to boil 1 cup to 1 pint of maple syrup until it smells burnt and is very dark or black in color; however, this process is very hard on cookware. Burnt sugar syrup can be kept in a jar for future use. Burnt sugar, an accident in the maple sugaring process—usually caused by an inattentive maker—was put to use in flavoring cakes.

Somerset Historical Center

Sweetcakes

1 cup New Orleans style molasses

2 tablespoons butter

1 tablespoon whiskey

2 teaspoons ground ginger

1/2 cup buttermilk

flour to make stiff dough, about 4 cups

1/2 teaspoon baking soda

1 egg white

1 tablespoon water

sugar

Heat molasses and butter until butter is melted. Allow to cool slightly, then add whiskey and ginger. Add buttermilk, then add flour and baking soda. The dough may be a little warm and soft at this time; place it in the refrigerator for about 1/2 hour. Then roll out fairly thin on a well-floured board. Cut with a cookie cutter, and place on lightly greased cookie sheet. Brush tops with egg wash (egg white and water combined), and sprinkle with sugar. Bake at 350 degrees for 10 to 12 minutes. Makes 100 small cookies. *Note:* This recipe is adapted from a broadside printed at Ephrata in 1824 by John Banmar.

Ephrata Cloister

U.S. Brig *Niagara* Birthday Brownies

4 ounces unsweetened baking chocolate

1 cup butter

4 large eggs

2 cups sugar

2 teaspoons vanilla

1 cup flour

3/4 cup walnuts, chopped

Grease 9x13-inch baking pan. Melt chocolate and butter together over low heat; set aside to cool slightly. Beat eggs and sugar together until frothy. Add vanilla to beaten eggs, and then slowly add chocolate mixture, blending well. Add flour and beat until smooth. Fold in walnuts. Spread batter in prepared pan and bake at 350 degrees for 25 to 30 minutes. Cool completely on wire rack.

Fudge Frosting

4 ounces unsweetened baking chocolate

2 cups sugar

2 large eggs, well beaten

1/4 cup light cream or half-and-half

1/4 cup butter

2 teaspoons vanilla

Melt chocolate over low heat in saucepan. Stir in sugar, eggs, cream, butter, and vanilla; blend well. Increase heat and bring to boil, stirring constantly. Remove from heat and cool slightly. Spread frosting over completely cooled brownies. Allow frosting to set before cutting into squares. Makes 8 to 12 servings. *Note:* These brownies, baked in the wood-burning stove on the *Niagara* are a special treat for the modern-day crew.

Erie Maritime Museum and U.S. Brig **Niagara**

Walnut Rocks

1 cup butter

1 1/2 cups brown sugar

3 eggs, beaten

1 teaspoon baking soda mixed into 1 1/2 tablespoons hot water

3 cups flour

1/2 teaspoon salt

1 teaspoon cinnamon

1/2 teaspoon cloves

1 1/2 cup raisins

1 cup chopped walnuts

Cream butter and sugar, and add beaten eggs. Dissolve soda in hot water and add to creamed mixture. Sift flour, salt, and spices together twice. Add half of this to mixture and mix thoroughly. Combine raisins and nuts with the other half and add to dough. Mix thoroughly. Drop by teaspoonfuls onto greased baking sheets spaced a couple inches apart. Bake at 350 degrees for 12 to15 minutes. Makes 4 dozen. *Note:* These were made by Mrs. Degn with black walnuts from Hope Lodge.

Hope Lodge

Gertrude Rapp Ginger Cookies

1/3 cup shortening

1 cup brown sugar, packed

1 1/2 cups dark molasses

2/3 cup cold water

6 cups flour

2 teaspoons baking soda

1 teaspoon salt

1 teaspoon allspice

1 teaspoon ginger

1 teaspoon cloves

1 teaspoon cinnamon

Cream shortening and sugar. Add molasses and water; add dry ingredients and mix well. Roll out about 1/2 inch thick. Cut with 2 1/2-inch round cutter. Place far apart on lightly greased cookie sheet. Bake at 350 degrees for 15 minutes, or until cookie springs back when touched, leaving no imprint. Makes about 30 fat, puffy cookies. *Note:* Gertrude was the granddaughter of George Rapp, the spiritual leader of the Harmony Society.

Old Economy Village

Ring-a-lings

1/2 cup butter or margarine

3 tablespoons confectioner's sugar

1 cup sifted flour

dash salt

1 cup finely chopped pecans

1 teaspoon vanilla

jam or jelly, any flavor

Cream together butter and confectioner's sugar. Stir in flour, salt, pecans, and vanilla. Chill several hours, or until firm enough to handle. Roll teaspoonfuls of dough into marble-size balls, and place 2 inches apart on ungreased cookie sheet. Make a hollow center in each with thumb, and fill with 1/2 teaspoon jam. Bake at 300 degrees for 20 minutes. Cool. Pack between waxed paper. Can be stored as long as 2 weeks. Makes 4 dozen cookies. *Note:* Made by Nancy Wentz Yambor, who was born in tenant house at Hope Lodge.

Hope Lodge

Applesauce Spice Cake

2³/₄ cups flour

2 cups sugar

¹/₄ teaspoon baking powder

1¹/₂ teaspoons baking soda

1¹/₂ teaspoons salt

³/₄ teaspoon cinnamon

¹/₂ teaspoon cloves

¹/₂ teaspoon allspice

¹/₂ cup soft margarine

¹/₂ cup water

1¹/₂ cups unsweetened applesauce

2 eggs

1 cup raisins

Sift flour into bowl with sugar, baking powder, baking soda, salt, and spices.
Add margarine, water, and applesauce. Beat in eggs, then add raisins. Pour
into a 13x9-inch pan. Bake at 350 degrees for 45 to 50 minutes.

Hope Lodge

Snickerdoodles

1¹/₃ cups plus 2 tablespoons sugar

1¹/₂ teaspoons cinnamon

1 cup margarine (room temperature)

2 eggs

3 cups flour

1¹/₂ teaspoons cream of tartar

1 teaspoon baking soda

Mix 2 tablespoons sugar and cinnamon, and set aside. Beat together margarine, 1¹/₃ cups sugar, and eggs until fluffy. Add flour, cream of tartar, and
baking soda until blended. Shape into 1-inch balls. Roll in cinnamon-sugar
topping, covering completely. Place 2¹/₂ inches apart on ungreased sheets.
Bake at 375 degrees for 10 minutes, or until golden brown. Cool on racks.
Makes about 3 dozen. *Note:* Made by Virginia Wentz Sinn, who was born
in tenant house at Hope Lodge.

Hope Lodge

FOOD PRESERVATION

Before the days of mechanical refrigeration, preservation of food was a time-consuming process that required considerable ingenuity, as well as the proper storage area or building. In many early homes, storage was found within the house. Hope Lodge, in Fort Washington, Montgomery County, features a root cellar—a shuttered cool and dry room—for storing potatoes, carrots, and other vegetables. The house also has a meat cellar with a plastered ceiling to keep odors from rising to the floor above, and a dairy cellar with a trough that held running water around three sides to cool the room through evaporation.

Other homes had separate springhouses, such as the one found at Conrad Weiser Homestead. The stone building was constructed on top of a spring, whose cold, clear water was used to chill perishable food items. At the Daniel Boone Homestead, the spring is found in the basement of the house—the foundation walls of the original Boone home—where the family used it as both their water source and a place to keep dairy products in earthen crocks immersed in the water. Although ice storage was not common in the seventeenth century, Pennsbury Manor's reconstructed icehouse almost certainly was stocked with sawdust-packed ice from the nearby Delaware River during the winter months.

When long-term preservation—particularly of meats or fish—was necessary, salt curing or smoking was employed. Smokehouses such as those at Pennsbury Manor and the Daniel Boone Homestead were constructed to smoke beef and pork. Meat hung from the joists, and a hickory or applewood fire was built on the dirt floor. Sawdust or leaves were heaped on the flames to produce smoke, which billowed out through the cracks and eaves of the smokehouse. It took about two weeks to smoke the meat, during which time the fire needed constant tending.

The meat cellar at Hope Lodge. CRAIG A. BENNER

Above: *The spring at the Daniel Boone Homestead.*
CRAIG A. BENNER

Right: *A World War II-era poster encouraging people to preserve fruits and vegetables.*
PENNSYLVANIA STATE ARCHIVES

Although a method for canning foods was developed in the eighteenth century, home canning was not widespread until John Mason patented his glass canning jar in 1858. Canning provided a means for storing meats, vegetables, fruits, and preserves over an extended period of time with little risk of spoilage. In many coal towns and mill towns, home gardens were sources of food not controlled by the company stores, and canning provided a means to extend the harvest. Canning experienced a revival during World Wars I and II, when victory gardens flourished and housewives sought ways to stretch the yield of their plots as far as possible. One poster of the period urged, "Can all you can. Food thrift—your patriotic duty."

Swedish Spritz Cookies

2 cups sifted flour
³/₄ cup sugar
2 egg yolks
I cup butter
I teaspoon almond extract

Sift together flour and sugar onto bread board. Make a well in the center, and drop in egg yolks, butter, and extract. Mix into a smooth dough with fingertips. Force through cookie press onto ungreased cookie sheets in O and S shapes. Bake in 375-degree oven for 8 to 10 minutes. Store in airtight container. Let cookies sit for a day to enhance the almond flavor. Makes 8 dozen cookies.

Morton Homestead

The dining room at Hope Lodge. CRAIG A. BENNER

Colonial Baked Pears

4 to 6 large, ripe, firm pears
thinly pared strips orange peel
4 to 6 tablespoons brown sugar
strained juice of 1 orange
1/2 to 3/4 cup port wine
2 whole cloves

Peel, halve, and core pears. Place cut-side-up in a heatproof dish. Lay one strip of orange peel in the hollow of each pear. Sprinkle 1 tablespoon brown sugar over each pear. Sprinkle orange juice over and around each pear. Combine wine and cloves. Pour into dish with pears. Bake in a 350-degree oven for 40 minutes, basting occasionally with wine. Serve warm or cold. Makes 8 to 12 servings.

Hope Lodge

Cream Sponge Cake

2 eggs

sour cream

1 cup sugar

juice and zest of 1 lemon

1 teaspoon cream of tartar

1/2 teaspoon baking soda

1 cup flour

Beat eggs in a 1 cup measure; fill up the cup with sour cream. Beat together in bowl with sugar and add lemon juice and zest. Mix cream of tartar and baking soda with flour. Stir into mixture. Place in small greased and floured bundt pan. Bake at 350 degrees for 20 to 25 minutes, or until done. *Note: This is an authentic recipe from* Mrs. Koechling's Receipt Book, 1850–1890.

Landis Valley Museum

Apple Butter Pie

1 egg, well beaten

3/4 cup apple butter

1 cup sugar

1 1/2 heaping tablespoons flour

1 teaspoon cinnamon

1/2 teaspoon nutmeg

1 teaspoon vanilla

1 cup milk

piecrust

Mix apple butter, sugar, and flour into beaten egg. Add milk to spices and flavoring and add to mixture. Pour into unbaked piecrust. Bake at 350 degrees about 35 to 40 minutes, until knife comes out clean. *Note:* Recipe is from Elizabeth Wessel Tospon (1852–1920), of Somerset County, handed down by family members.

Somerset Historical Center

Baked Indian Pudding

3 cups milk
1/2 cup yellow cornmeal
5 eggs
pinch baking soda
1/2 cup dark molasses
1/2 cup seedless raisins
1 teaspoon grated lemon rind
1/2 teaspoon ginger
1 teaspoon cinnamon
4 tablespoons butter
1 teaspoon salt
1/4 cup sugar
1 cup cold milk

In double boiler, bring milk to the scald. Add cornmeal, stirring constantly until mixture thickens, about 10 minutes. Remove from heat and set aside to cool partially. Meanwhile, beat eggs until lemon color, and stir baking soda into molasses. Now, into partially cooled cornmeal, stir raisins, lemon rind, ginger, cinnamon, butter, molasses–baking soda mixture, salt, sugar, and beaten eggs. Pour mixture into greased baking dish. Stir in cold milk. Bake in a 275-degree oven until cooked through, about 3 hours. Serve hot with fruit sauce. Makes 8 servings.

Fruit Sauce

1 small can pineapple tidbits
1 orange
1 apple
1 1/2 cups water
1 cup sugar
juice of 1 lemon

Drain juice from pineapple into saucepan. Peel orange, remove membrane, and cut sections into 3 pieces each. Core, peel, and dice apple into 1/4-inch pieces. Stir water, sugar, and lemon juice into pineapple juice, and bring to a boil. Add fruit to boiling syrup, reduce heat, and simmer for 10 minutes, until thickened. *Note:* A popular dessert on the Erie Railroad.

Railroad Museum of Pennsylvania

Scotch Shortbread

1 pound butter

1 cup powdered sugar

3 cups sifted flour

1 cup rice flour or 3/4 cup cornstarch

Cream butter and add sugar gradually. Blend well, but don't overwork it or let butter become oily. Gradually work in flour and rice flour or cornstarch. Turn dough out on lightly floured board (you may use part confectioner's sugar and part flour to "flour" your board). For a traditional look, pat the dough into two circles, about 3/4 inch thick. Pinch edges, and prick all over with fork. Place on baking sheet. Put shortbread in refrigerator or freezer for 1/2 hour. Then bake at 375 degrees for 5 minutes. Lower the temperature to 300 degrees, and continue baking for 45 to 60 minutes more. When done, shortbread should be golden, but not browned at all. Cut into wedges while still warm. Makes about 32 servings.

Washington Crossing Historic Park

Taffy for Pulling

1 cup sugar

1/2 cup dark Karo syrup

1/2 cup cold water

1 teaspoon vinegar

1 tablespoon butter

Put sugar, syrup, water, and vinegar in saucepan over low heat. Stir until sugar is completely dissolved. Boil on high heat. Add butter when it reaches a rolling boil. This settles it to an even boil. From time to time, drop by teaspoon into tin of cold water. (*Important:* Do not stir while boiling; carefully dip by spoonful to test.) When syrup spins a brittle thread when dropped in ice water, remove at once from stove. Pour into lightly buttered pan. Cool till it can be gathered into ball in center of pan. It will be ready to pull when cool enough to handle. Pull and twist until it turns somewhat white and creamy in color. Cut into bite-size pieces with scissors. Makes 1 pound. *Note:* Recipe was given to Loris Bowlby by Jenny Boose Good of Somerset around 1930. Mrs. Good was in her eighties at that time. She often invited her Sunday school students to her house for taffy pulls and pulled taffy before her card games so the ladies would have something to munch on when playing cards.

Somerset Historical Center

English Fruitcake

I pound butter
I pound brown sugar
10 eggs, beaten
I pint strawberry preserves
I pint molasses
I rounded teaspoon baking soda
2 teaspoons salt
I teaspoon cinnamon
I teaspoon ginger
I teaspoon allspice
I teaspoon nutmeg
$^{1}/_{2}$ teaspoon ground cloves
7 cups flour
3 pounds raisins
3 pounds currants
I pound dates
$^{1}/_{2}$ pound citron
$^{1}/_{2}$ pound lemon peel
$^{1}/_{2}$ pound orange peel
I cup good brandy or sherry (optional)

Cream together butter and brown sugar. Mix in eggs, strawberry preserves, molasses, baking soda, salt, and spices. Add flour and beat. Mix in fruits and blend well. Pour into 2 10-inch springform tube pans lined with greased brown paper or cooking parchment. Bake at 300 degrees for 2 to 2$^{1}/_{2}$ hours. Wrap cakes in cheesecloth. Paint with brandy or sherry if desired. Store in crock or tin in a cool place for at least 2 weeks before slicing. Makes 2 fruitcakes.

Washington Crossing Historic Park

Maple Sugar Pie #I

3 eggs
2 cups maple sugar
2 cups white sugar
I2 tablespoons flour
3 cups milk
melted butter
piecrust

Beat eggs; add sugars, flour, milk, and a little melted butter. Pour into unbaked piecrust. Bake at 350 degrees for about 30 minutes, until inserted knife comes out clean. *Note:* Recipe is from Laura Freidline, who made this pie during the 1920s at her home in Lambertsville, Somerset County.

Somerset Historical Center

Maple Sugar Pie #2

3/4 **cup maple sugar (brown sugar will also work)**

3/4 **cup white sugar**

2 **rounded tablespoons flour**

1 **cup whole milk**

piecrust

butter

cinnamon

Mix first four ingredients together and pour into unbaked piecrust. Dot with butter and sprinkle cinnamon over top. Bake at 350 degrees for about 30 to 35 minutes, until inserted knife comes out clean.

Somerset Historical Center

Mixed Fruit Brulee

3 **tablespoons sugar, or to taste**

6 **tablespoons water**

1 **tablespoon lemon juice**

1 1/2 **to 2 pounds mixed fresh or frozen fruits: strawberries, peaches, bananas, apples, pears, grapes, etc.**

10 **ounces whipping cream**

4 **tablespoons dark brown sugar**

Dissolve sugar in water in a small saucepan. Stir in lemon juice and remove from heat. Put prepared fruits into a flameproof serving dish, and stir in sugar syrup. Press fruit down to level the top. Whip cream until stiff, and spread over fruit. Chill until just before serving. To serve, sprinkle brown sugar over cream, and place under broiler until sugar melts—only 1 or 2 minutes. Serve immediately. Makes 4 to 6 servings. *Note:* You can add 1 or 2 tablespoons of your favorite liquor to the fruit for additional flavor. Reduce quantity of water by like amount.

Joseph Priestley House

MAPLE SUGAR AND SYRUP

No one can be certain when or how the sweet taste of maple sap was discovered, or how the Native Americans learned to boil it into syrup and sugar, but there is little doubt that native people taught frontiersmen how to produce it. By 1790, maple sugaring was an established industry in Pennsylvania and provided a winter "crop" for many farmers during their slow season. A sugar maple could produce 2 to 3 gallons of liquid per day, which farmers collected into horse-drawn tanks. The sap was boiled over a fire into syrup, some of which was stirred into sugar that would harden into a cake. Further stirring caused it to form granules. The procedure required little equipment at the sugar camps, which remained relatively primitive, as they were used for only a brief period each year. Later, primitive sheds were built, some with a cupola in the roof to vent the steam.

Much of the early production ended up as maple sugar, which was easier to transport and could be converted back to syrup after reaching its destination. A less costly alternative to cane sugar, maple sugar became an important commodity used for sweetening or curing food. During the late nineteenth century, when cane sugar became available at a competitive price, farmers began to market maple syrup as a perfect complement to pancakes (page 25) or griddle cakes (page 30) and other foods. Today maple syrup, maple candy, and dishes made with maple products,

Collecting maple sap. PENNSYLVANIA STATE ARCHIVES

Making maple syrup and sugar. PENNSYLVANIA STATE ARCHIVES

such as maple sugar pie (pages 108 and 109) and burnt sugar cake (page 97), continue to be popular.

In 1992, the Somerset Historical Center in Somerset County constructed a historically accurate replica of a mid-nineteenth-century sugar camp, featuring authentic maple sugar–making tools and equipment from the center's collection. Somerset County still leads the commonwealth in the production of maple sugar products.

Above: *Boiling syrup to make maple sugar in Somerset County, 1934.* PENNSYLVANIA STATE ARCHIVES

Left: *Tending a kettle of maple sugar in Somerset County, 1934.* PENNSYLVANIA STATE ARCHIVES

LEVITTOWN'S KITCHEN
OF THE FUTURE

After World War II, demand for new homes by returning GIs far outstripped the tight housing market. Alfred and William Levitt pioneered the affordable suburban housing development by developing a system of preassembled sections and components, which were built on concrete slabs in an assembly-line routine. After completing the first Levittown on Long Island in New York, the Levitt brothers bought land in Bucks County, Pennsylvania. The houses built by Levitt and Sons became part of the largest planned community in the country. This new suburb, with affordable prices, was built to provide housing for workers in the Philadelphia area, including U.S. Steel's Fairless Works, which opened nearby in 1952. The new suburbs combined country comforts with city conveniences. With the help of modern production and financing methods, builders like Levitt and Sons made the American dream of homeownership affordable to millions.

Brochures for Levittown promised, "Any home you select in Levittown will give you the comforts and conveniences that take the drudgery out of housekeeping." The kitchens reflected the "modern efficiency" of the new suburb and featured all major appliances, including an automatic washer and dryer. General Electric outfitted all of Levittown's homes. With the built-in kitchen, no space went to waste. Gone were the antiseptic white kitchens of earlier eras, replaced by pastels. Homeowners could also choose options like a built-in push-button "food center" with interchangeable mixer, knife sharpener, and blender attachments. A complete Levittown kitchen is in the collections of The State Museum in Harrisburg, Dauphin County.

Levittown also had a modern supermarket in the Shop-a-rama shopping center, which featured the newest in packaged foods designed to entice the housewife—instant coffee, frozen pot pies, and TV dinners. The supermarket also offered recipes such as chicken with rice and apricot stuffing (page 62) to encourage shoppers to buy additional products at the store.

Original Levittown kitchen, 1958. DON GILES/THE STATE MUSEUM OF PENNSYLVANIA

Spiced Bran Muffins

I cup flour

2 cups bran flakes, crushed

1 1/2 teaspoons baking powder

I teaspoon cinnamon

1/4 teaspoon salt

1/4 teaspoon nutmeg

I beaten egg

I cup milk

1/2 cup dark brown sugar, packed

1/4 cup cooking oil

I teaspoon finely shredded orange peel

1/2 cup chopped pecans

6 ounces whole cranberries

In large mixing bowl, stir together flour, bran cereal, baking powder, cinnamon, salt, and nutmeg. Make a well in center. In another mixing bowl, stir together egg, milk, brown sugar, oil, and orange peel. Add egg mixture all at once to flour mixture. Stir until moistened (batter will be lumpy). Fold in nuts. Gently fold in cranberries. Grease muffin cups or line with paper bake cups; fill 2/3 full. Bake in 400-degree oven for 15 to 20 minutes, or until muffins are golden. Makes 12 muffins.

The State Museum of Pennsylvania

Rhubarb Crumble

2 pounds rhubarb, sliced into 1/2-inch or smaller slices

1/2 to 3/4 cup sugar, or to taste

2 teaspoons grated fresh ginger

I cup flour

I teaspoon baking powder

1/4 pound butter, room temperature

1 1/4 cups oatmeal

4 ounces brown sugar

Stew rhubarb, sugar, and ginger over low heat for 15 minutes, or until soft. Put in baking dish. Mix together flour and baking powder, and blend in butter. Add oatmeal and brown sugar. Spread mixture over rhubarb. Bake in preheated 350-degree oven for 30 minutes. Makes 6 to 8 servings.

Joseph Priestley House

Beverages

Mrs. Degn's Spiced Tea

16 cups water, divided
1¹/₂ cups sugar
1 tablespoon whole cloves
5 tablespoons tea
juice of 8 oranges
juice of 1 lemon

Boil sugar and cloves in 8 cups water. Add tea to 8 more cups boiling water, and steep for 3 to 5 minutes. Combine with sugar and clove water. Stir in fruit juices, heat briefly, then serve. Makes 25 servings.

Hope Lodge

May's Punch

juice of 3 dozen lemons
2 quarts strong tea
4 quarts orange juice
3 46-ounce cans and 1 11.5-ounce can pineapple juice
2 pounds sugar made into syrup with 4 cups water
20-ounce can shredded or chopped pineapple
3 quarts ginger ale
raspberry juice for flavor (optional)

Mix together first five ingredients. Add ice 15 minutes before serving. Add ginger ale just before serving. Makes 70 servings. *Note:* This punch was also made by Mrs. Degn, last private owner of Hope Lodge.

Hope Lodge

Left: *Daniel Boone Homestead.* CRAIG A. BENNER

Root Beer

7 cups distilled or purified water
1 1/2 cups white sugar
1/4 teaspoon active dry yeast
1 teaspoon root beer concentrate

Measure water into a glass bowl and heat in a microwave on high for 3 minutes. You can also heat water in a nonaluminum pan on a stove burner until lukewarm. Do not overheat it, though, or it will deactivate yeast. Add sugar, yeast, and root beer concentrate to the water, and stir slowly until sugar and yeast dissolve. Place a small plastic funnel in mouth of a 2-liter plastic bottle. Using a small cup or ladle, pour soda mixture through funnel. Fill bottle, leaving 2 to 3 inches of air at top. Remove funnel, and screw bottle cap on tightly. If air leaks out, root beer will not carbonate properly. Lay filled bottle on its side in a warm place, and leave undisturbed for 4 days. During this time, root beer will carbonate as sugar and yeast react to form tiny carbon dioxide bubbles that give soda its fizz. On the fifth day, put root beer in refrigerator to chill. It will be ready to drink the following day. Makes 2 liters.

Note: The best way to serve your homemade root beer is in frosted glass mugs. As you unscrew the bottle cap, listen for the soft *whoosh* sound as the pressurized air at the top of the bottle escapes. When you pour the root beer, you should see bubbles on the side of the glass and foam forming at the top. You'll notice a slight yeasty flavor to your homemade brew, as well as a hint of anise and wintergreen. If the flavor is too strong, just add a small amount of cold water. Or make a root beer float by adding a scoop of ice cream or frozen yogurt; vanilla tastes especially good.

Joseph Priestley House

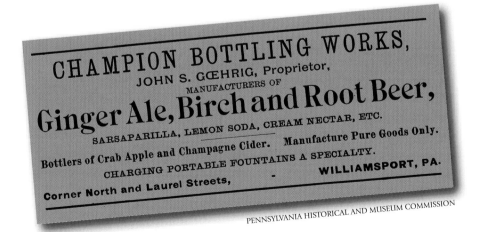

CHAMPION BOTTLING WORKS,
JOHN S. GŒHRIG, Proprietor,
MANUFACTURERS OF
Ginger Ale, Birch and Root Beer,
SARSAPARILLA, LEMON SODA, CREAM NECTAR, ETC.
Bottlers of Crab Apple and Champagne Cider.   Manufacture Pure Goods Only.
CHARGING PORTABLE FOUNTAINS A SPECIALTY.
Corner North and Laurel Streets,   -   WILLIAMSPORT, PA.

PRIESTLEY PUTS THE POP
IN SODA POP

Joseph Priestley (1733–1804) was an English theologian, teacher, and natural philosopher who in 1794 settled in Northumberland, Pennsylvania, where he built a home complete with a chemical laboratory for carrying out his continuing work in science. Today the Joseph Priestley House in Northumberland County showcases his life and his work.

Most often recognized for discovering the element oxygen in 1774 while living in Calne, England, Priestley is also hailed for his description of the process of carbonation, for which the Royal Society awarded him its highly desired Copley Prize in 1773. Priestley's "sparkling" discovery is said by many to have led to the development of the modern soft-drink industry. In 1767, the first drinkable man-made glass of carbonated water was created by Priestley. The manufacture of soft drinks didn't begin until the 1830s, however, with the introduction of bottled soda water, some flavored with birch bark, dandelions, sarsaparilla, and fruit extracts. In 1861, the term "pop" was first coined. Root beer (page 116) was mass produced by 1876, and in 1881, the first cola-flavored beverage was introduced. Eighteenth-century science has been translated into a twentieth-century institution, thanks to Joseph Priestley.

Martha Washington's Rum Punch

1 orange, quartered

3 lemons, quartered

3 cinnamon sticks, broken

6 cloves

1/2 teaspoon grated nutmeg

4 ounces simple syrup

4 ounces lemon juice

4 ounces fresh orange juice

12 ounces boiling water

3 ounces white rum

3 ounces dark rum

3 ounces orange curaçao

lemon and orange wheels (for garnish)

In a container, mash the orange, lemons, cinnamon sticks, cloves, and nutmeg. Add syrup and lemon and orange juices. Pour boiling water over mixture. Let cool. When cool, add white rum, dark rum, and orange curaçao. Strain well into a pitcher or punch bowl. Serve over ice in goblets. Decorate with wheels of lemon and orange. Makes 6 to 10 servings.

Washington Crossing Historic Park

PUBLIC HOUSES

I f some early Pennsylvania colonists had had their way, taverns, also known as "ordinaries," would not have been part of Philadelphia's landscape. Taverns in England had a reputation of being hotbeds of corruption, public drunkenness, and political chicanery. Taverns were constructed in Philadelphia even before William Penn arrived in the city, though Penn was determined to license tavern owners, control prices, and insist on a certain degree of propriety.

While taverns in cities and towns became the social and political gathering places for local citizens, other taverns, often nothing more than log cabins or farmhouses, were built along roads for travelers. To the traveler, the tavern represented a hot meal and a place to rest at night during the six or seven days it took a horse and rider to travel between Philadelphia and Pittsburgh. A change of horses, a blacksmith, and a wheelwright might also be available for the travelers' Conestoga wagons and carriages. There were about sixty taverns between Lancaster and Philadelphia by 1840, and each was a place at which rural citizens could catch up on the news of the growing nation.

The dinner meal, consisting generally of two courses, might include beef, game, fish, poultry

Above: *Tavern-cooking at Landis Valley Museum.* CRAIG A. BENNER

Right: *Landis Valley tavern interior.*
CRAIG A. BENNER

(see pork and chicken soup, page 10), puddings, fruit pies, breads, jellies, and pickled foods, such as red beet eggs (page 5). Coffee, tea, liquor, soup, and even ice cream were available at the bar at all times. After the main courses, the tablecloth was often removed, and fruit, cheese, and wine were offered. Travelers of lesser means could expect a more modest menu at rural taverns.

At the Landis Valley Museum in Lancaster County, visitors can explore the Landis Valley House Hotel (1855–56), a two-story country hotel where local residents and travelers ate their meals and visited the barroom, and the Tavern Building, constructed in 1940 and furnished and interpreted as an early-nineteenth-century tavern. The eating area and kitchen of the tavern feature tableware and cooking equipment, including toasters, waffle irons, cast-iron pots, wrought-iron ladles, strainers, skimmers, rolling pins, wooden bowls, redware plates, and stoneware jugs. These items are used in demonstrations showcasing nineteenth-century cooking methods, unique sensory visits to the past.

McConkey Ferry Inn at Washington Crossing Historic Park. CRAIG A. BENNER

Wine Syllabub from Philadelphia

3/4 cup sugar

3 tablespoons lemon juice

I cup sherry, Madeira, or port

I pint heavy cream, whipped

cinnamon

nutmeg

sponge cake

In a cut-glass bowl, mix sugar with lemon juice and wine. When dissolved, carefully fold in whipped cream. Serve very cold in glasses (sherbet glasses are perfect), first putting a square of wine-soaked sponge cake in bottom of each glass. Sprinkle top with cinnamon and nutmeg. Makes 8 servings.

Hope Lodge

Fish House Punch

2 cups lemon juice (I pint)

18 cups water (9 pints)

4 pounds superfine sugar

1/2 gallon Jamaican rum

I quart cognac brandy

I quart peach brandy

ice ring

2 to 3 lemons, sliced

Dissolve sugar in water and lemon juice in large punch bowl. Add liquors, and cover bowl with plastic. Refrigerate for four hours. Just before serving, add ice ring and float lemon slices for garnish. Serves 50.

Pennsylvania State Archives

Cherry Bounce

I pound fresh cherries, pitted

I cup plus 2 tablespoons sugar or 1/2 pound rock candy

11/2 cups brandy

Place all ingredients in clean, scalded, glass-topped quart jar or apothecary jar, and cover tightly. Let stand 3 months in a cool place. Stir or shake occasionally to dissolve sugar or rock candy. Since sugar tends to settle, make sure it is getting thoroughly mixed. Taste occasionally to make sure it is sweet enough, adding more sugar as needed. Strain into glasses. Makes 6 servings.

The State Museum of Pennsylvania

Egg Punch (Eggnog)

6 eggs, separated
$3/4$ cup sugar
pinch salt
6 cups whole milk
I teaspoon vanilla
$3/4$ cup whipping cream
rum (optional)
nutmeg

Beat egg yolks, sugar, and salt in top of double boiler. Add milk and mix well. Cook over hot water until mixture coats spoon, stirring frequently. Add vanilla. Chill. Beat egg whites until stiff. Beat whipping cream until stiff. Fold egg whites and whipping cream into custard mixture. Add rum if desired. Top with grated nutmeg. Makes 12 to 14 servings.

Old Economy Village

Ginger Beer

3 lemons
I $1/2$ pounds sugar
3 ounces ginger root, grated
2 gallons boiling water
I teaspoon ($1/2$ packet) wine yeast

Squeeze juice from lemons, strain, and set aside. Mix together sugar, grated ginger, and the peelings from 2 lemons. Put mixture in a pot or crock, and pour boiling water over it. When mixture becomes lukewarm, strain it, and add strained juice from 3 squeezed lemons and yeast. Let mixture sit overnight, or 12 hours, then pour the ginger beer into 20-ounce plastic bottles (water bottles are ideal), leaving about $1 1/2$ inches head room. Let sit in warm place for 72 hours, then place bottles in cool place. Should be refrigerated after 1 week to stop any further carbonation. May drink beer after 3 days. Tastes best chilled. Makes 14 to 15 20-ounce bottles. *Note:* Buy bottled water, use the water to make the ginger beer, and you have the proper size clean containers for bottling.

Old Economy Village

Pennsylvania
Trail of History

Anthracite Heritage Museum and Scranton Iron Furnaces

R.D. #1, Bald Mountain Road
Scranton, PA 18504
570-963-4804
www.anthracitemuseum.org

The museum that explores the lives and labors of the people of Pennsylvania's hard coal region and site of the iron furnaces that relied on anthracite to roll the rails of the nation.

Brandywine Battlefield Park

U.S. Route 1
Box 202
Chadds Ford, PA 19317
610-459-3342
www.ushistory.org/brandywine

The park that commemorates the largest battle of the American Revolution, pitting George Washington's troops against William Howe's advancing British forces.

Bushy Run Battlefield

PA Route 993 (near Jeannette)
Box 468
Harrison City, PA 15636
724-527-5584
www.bushyrunbattlefield.com

The site of the 1763 encounter between British and Native American forces that decided the territorial fate of the Pennsylvania frontier

Conrad Weiser Homestead

28 Weiser Road
Womelsdorf, PA 19567
610-589-2934
www.phmc.state.pa.us

The park that commemorates the Colonial diplomat who mediated peace between Pennsylvania an the powerful Iroquois Nation prior to the French and Indian War.

Left: *Bushy Run Battlefield.* ART BECKER

Cornwall Iron Furnace

Rexmont Road and Boyd Street
Box 251
Cornwall, PA 17016
717-272-9711
www.phmc.state.pa.us
   The site that for a century and a half was the heart of a vast industrial plantation and is now a landmark of Pennsylvania's iron industry.

Daniel Boone Homestead

400 Daniel Boone Road
Birdsboro, PA 19508
610-582-4900
www.danielboonehomestead.org
   The site of the legendary pioneer's birth in 1734, offering a unique glimpse at early Pennsylvania settlement.

Drake Well Museum and Park

202 Museum Lane
Titusville, PA 16354
814-827-2797
www.drakewell.org
   The museum that preserves Pennsylvania's petroleum heritage on the site where Edwin L. Drake drilled oil in 1859, launching the modern oil industry.

Eckley Miners' Village

R.D. #2, Box 236 (off PA Route 940)
Weatherly, PA 18255
570-636-2070
www.phmc.state.pa.us
   The patch town that was home to anthracite coal mine workers and their families for more than 100 years.

Ephrata Cloister

632 West Main Street (U.S. Route 322)
Ephrata, PA 17522
717-733-6600
www.phmc.state.pa.us
   The site of a unique eighteenth-century religious society, known for its original music and *Fraktur*, distinctive medieval-style architecture, and prolific publishing center.

Erie Maritime Museum

150 East Front Street
Erie, PA 16507
814-452-2744
www.brigniagara.org/museum.htm
   The museum that interprets the 1813 Battle of Lake Erie and Erie's maritime heritage and serves as homeport for U.S. Brig *Niagara*.

Fort Pitt Museum

101 Commonwealth Place
Pittsburgh, PA 15222
412-281-9285
www.fortpittmuseum.com
   The museum that unfolds the saga of the bitter struggle through the eightennth century for control of North America.

Graeme Park

859 County Line Road
Horsham, PA 19044
215-343-0965
www.ushistory.org/graeme
   The mysterious mansion that was first the residence of provincial Pennsylvania governor Sir William Keith, then prominent physician Thomas Graeme, and later literary figure Elizabeth Graeme Ferguson.

Hope Lodge and Mather Mill

553 South Bethlehem Pike
Fort Washington, PA 19034
215-646-1595
www.ushistory.org/hope
   One of the finest surviving Georgian homes, furnished in the styles of both the Colonial era and the early-twentieth-century Colonial Revival.

Joseph Priestley House

472 Priestley Avenue
Northumberland, PA 17857
570-473-9474
www.phmc.state.pa.us
   The American home and laboratory of the founder of modern chemistry and discoverer of oxygen.

Landis Valley Museum

2451 Kissel Hill Road (PA Route 272)
Lancaster, PA 17601
717-569-0401
www.landisvalleymuseum.org
   The museum complex that interprets traditional Pennsylvania Dutch rural life through an exceptional collection of objects, historic buildings, and demonstrations of crafts, farming, and domestic practices.

Morton Homestead

100 Lincoln Avenue
Prospect Park, PA 19076
610-583-7221
www.phmc.state.pa.us
   The site of one of the earliest Swedish settlements in Pennsylvania and memorial to John Morton, signer of the Declaration of Independence.

Museum of Anthracite Mining

17th and Pine Streets
Ashland, PA 17921
570-875-4708
www.phmc.state.pa.us
    The museum that features a diverse collection of tools, machinery, and photographs depicting the anthracite coal industry in Pennsylvania.

Old Economy Village

270 Sixteenth Street
Ambridge, PA 15003
724-266-4500
www.oldeconomyvillage.org
    The last home of the Harmonists, a nineteenth-century Christian communal society known for its piety and industrial prosperity.

Pennsbury Manor

400 Pennsbury Memorial Lane
Morrisville, PA 19067
215-946-0400
www.pennsburymanor.org
    The reconstructed home of William Penn—America's foremost Quaker, founder of Pennsylvania, statesman, and diplomat.

Pennsylvania Lumber Museum

5660 U.S. Route 6 West
Box 239
Galeton, PA 16922
814-435-2652
www.lumbermuseum.org
    The outdoor museum that preserves the heritage of the early lumber industry in Pennsylvania.

Pennsylvania Military Museum

South Atherton Street (Business Route 322)
Box 160A
Boalsburg, PA 16827
814-466-6263
www.psu.edu/dept/aerospace/museum
    The museum that recounts the story of Pennsylvania's citizen soldiers—the men and women who served their country in time of war.

Railroad Museum of Pennsylvania

Route 741 East
Box 15
Strasburg, PA 17579
717-687-8628
www.rrmuseumpa.org
    The world-class museum that exhibits an extensive collection of locomotives, railcars, and equipment from Pennsylvania's historic railroads.

Somerset Historical Center

10649 Somerset Pike (PA Route 985)
Somerset, PA 15501
814-445-6077
www.somersethistoricalcenter.org
    Western Pennsylvania's rural heritage museum that recalls the fervent spirit that settled the Pennsylvania frontier.

The State Museum of Pennsylvania

300 North Street
Harrisburg, PA 17120
717-783-9911
www.statemuseumpa.org
    The museum of Pennsylvania's heritage from the earth's beginnings to the present, including archaeological artifacts, planetarium, fine art, decorative arts, dioramas, industrial and technological innovations, and military history.

U.S. Brig Niagara

150 East Front Street
Erie, PA 16507
814-452-2744
www.brigniagara.org
    Pennsylvania's historic flagship, a faithful reconstruction of the brig that carried Oliver Hazard Perry's fleet to victory in the Battle of Lake Erie.

Washington Crossing Historic Park

1112 River Road
Box 103
Washington Crossing, PA 18977
215-493-4076
www.phmc.state.pa.us
    The site where George Washington and his troops crossed the icy Delaware River on Christmas 1776 before their victory at Trenton.

Also Available

The Pennsylvania Trail of History Guides is a series of handbooks on the historic sites and museums administered by the Pennsylvania Historical and Museum Commission. Each handbook focuses on a particular site, offering a concise history of the subject and a detailed tour of the grounds, complete with full-color photos.

Anthracite Heritage Museum & Scranton Iron Furnaces
text by Harold W. Aurand
0-8117-2959-1

Brandywine Battlefield Park
text by Thomas J. McGuire; photos by Craig A. Benner
0-8117-2605-3

Bushy Run Battlefield
text by David Dixon; photos by Art Becker
0-8117-2890-0

Conrad Weiser Homestead
text by John Bradley; photos by Kyle R. Weaver
0-8117-2739-4

Cornwall Iron Furnace
text by Sue Dieffenbach; photos by Craig A. Benner
0-8117-2624-X

Daniel Boone Homestead
text by Sharon Hernes Silverman; photos by Craig A. Benner & Kyle R. Weaver
0-8117-2732-7

Drake Well Museum & Park
text by Jon Sherman; photos by Art Becker
0-8117-2960-5

Eckley Miners' Village
text by Perry Blatz; photos by Craig A. Benner
0-8117-2741-6

Ephrata Cloister
text by John Bradley; photos by Craig A. Benner
0-8117-2744-0

Erie Maritime Museum & U.S. Brig Niagara
text by Chris J. Magoc
0-8117-2756-4

Fort Pitt Museum
text by David Dixon
0-8117-2972-9

Graeme Park
text by Lorett Treese; photos by Kyle R. Weaver
0-8117-2785-8

Hope Lodge & Mather Mill
text by Lorett Treese; photos by Craig A. Benner and Kyle R. Weaver
0-8117-2471-9

Joseph Priestley House
text by Alison Duncan Hirsch; photos by Kyle R. Weaver
0-8117-2629-0

Landis Valley Museum
text by Elizabeth Johnson; photos by Craig A. Benner
0-8117-2955-9

Old Economy Village
text by Daniel B Reibel; photos by Art Becker
0-8117-2957-5

Pennsbury Manor
text by Larry E. Tise; photos by David J. Healy
0-8117-2910-9

Railroad Museum Of Pennsylvania
text by Dan Cupper
0-8117-2956-7

Somerset Historical Center
text by Lorett Treese
0-8117-3142-1

Washington Crossing Historic Park
text by John Bradley; photos by Craig A. Benner
0-8117-2885-4

COMING IN 2005

Pennsylvania Lumber Museum
text by Robert Currin; photos by Art Becker

Pennsylvania Military Museum
text by Arthur P. Miller Jr. and Marjorie L. Miller

The State Museum Of Pennsylvania
text by Sharon Hernes Silverman

All titles are $10, plus shipping,
from Stackpole Books, 800-732-3669, www.stackpolebooks.com, or
The Pennsylvania Historical and Museum Commission, 800-747-7790,
www.phmc.state.pa.us